The Classic Rice Cookbook

THE CLASSIC RICE COOKBOOK

Junko Takagi

SHUFUNOTOMO/JAPAN PUBLICATIONS

First printing, 1996

© Copyright in Japan 1996 by Junko Takagi
Photographs by Yoji Yamada
                     Johnny Hymas (pages: 4, 8-9)
Book Design by Office 21

Published by SHUFUNOTOMO CO., LTD.
2-9, Kanda Surugadai, Chiyoda-ku, Tokyo, 101 Japan

DISTRIBUTORS
United States: Kodansha America, Inc., through Farrar,
Straus & Giroux, 19 Union Square West, New York, NY
10003.
Canada: Fitzhenry & Whiteside Ltd., 195 Allstate
Parkway, Markham, Ontario L3R 4T8.
United Kingdom and Europe: Premier Book Marketing
Ltd., 1 Gower Street, London WC1E 6HA.
Australia and New Zealand: Bookwise International, 54
Crittenden Road, Findon, South Australia 5023.
The Far East and Japan: Japan Publications Trading Co.,
Ltd.,
1-2-1, Sarugaku-cho, Chiyoda-ku, Tokyo 101, Japan

ISBN: 0-87040-968-9
Printed in Hong Kong

PREFACE

Rice is the main staple of the Japanese diet. Because Japanese people grow up eating rice everyday, they develop a refined taste for it. Although Japan is a small country, it produces many different varieties of rice, which differ subtly in stickiness and sweetness. Japanese people choose rice based on their own tastes as well as its appropriateness for specific dishes.

With the increasing influence of foreign cuisines these days, the eating habits of Japanese people have been changing. Despite this trend, one or two meals a day continue to be in the traditional Japanese style for most people. A traditional Japanese meal consists of a variety of dishes served along with rice, which makes up fifty percent of the meal.

Rice has excellent nutritional value and a long shelf-life. One of its virtues is that its flavor is slightly sweet and yet rather bland, so it can be served with any kind of dish or it can be prepared as a dish of its own with any flavor.

Rice is wonderfully versatile; there are unlimited ways to prepare and enjoy it. In this cookbook, I have carefully selected recipes from a wide variety of rice dishes which I enjoy preparing often. I have included recipes for home-style standards which are still popular today, many kinds of sushi recipes, and rice dishes which feature seasonal vegetables. I have also included rice dishes from other countries—recipes from Southeast Asia and China, where rice is also the main staple, as well as recipes for Western-style rice dishes featuring Western ingredients. My hope is that through this cookbook, everyone—people around the world, from Asia and beyond—will come to take pleasure in eating rice.

Junko Takagi

CONTENTS

What Kind of Food is Rice?

Kinds of Rice and Their Characteristics: Japonica and Indica Rice

Rice is roughly divided into two types—Japonica and Indica. The characteristics and forms of these two types of rice differ.

Japonica rice is usually grown in temperate climates. The grains are round and do not easily crack or break. When cooked, this rice is sticky and moist. The rice produced in Japan is mostly Japonica. Many types of Japonica are also grown in Northern China, the Korean Peninsula and Taiwan. America has recently begun growing Japonica rice as well.

Indica rice is usually grown in hot climates. The grains are long and tend to break easily. When cooked, the rice is fluffy and does not stick together. Most of the rice produced in Southern Asia, including India, Thailand, Vietnam and Southern China, is Indica rice.

There are two methods of growing rice. One uses an irrigated field, while the other uses a dry rice field. In Japan, ninety-nine percent of all the rice produced is grown using irrigation. In Southeast Asia, dry rice fields are also used for growing rice. The grains of rice produced in dry rice fields tend to be thin, long and larger than rice grown in irrigated fields.

Non-Glutinous and Glutinous Rice

Both Japonica and Indica types of rice include non-glutinous and glutinous rice. Each type of rice has its own special characteristics and each has its own place in rice cooking.

Non-glutinous rice is popularly used in general rice cooking. This rice is somewhat transparent and when cooked is less sticky than glutinous rice. When the term "rice" is used in Japan, it refers to non-glutinous rice. Ninety-five percent of the rice harvested in Japan is non-glutinous. This rice is usually cooked in water and served plain. It is also used to make *miso* (soybean paste), saké (Japanese rice wine) and Japanese rice snacks.

Glutinous rice tends to be white and opaque and is very sticky when cooked. In Japan, glutinous rice is steamed or boiled and is referred to as *okowa* (for an example of a dish made with *okowa*, see page 28). It is also used to make rice cakes and processed to make rice snacks.

Brown Rice and Polished Rice

Rice is usually threshed and polished after harvesting. Rice which has simply been harvested and threshed is brown rice. Brown rice does not cook well in an ordinary pot, so often a pressure cooker is used. It requires more chewing and is harder to digest than white rice. However, brown rice can be stored longer than white rice and the original nutrients are preserved.

Semi-polished rice, which still has the whole

germ, is similar in nutritional value to brown rice. It contains most of the grain's original vitamins B_1, B_2 and E and can be prepared using conventional methods.

Polished rice, the type of rice generally consumed, has had the husk and bran completely removed. The terms "half-polished," "seventy-percent-polished" and "white rice" refer to the level of processing involved.

Most of the rice sold is white rice, which has had ninety percent of the rice bran removed.

Just as Europeans and Americans often have bread with their meals, rice is the main staple of the Japanese diet. Japanese therefore are quite discerning about rice. Many Japanese prefer rice which is sticky and slightly sweet. Rice is grown throughout Japan—from Hokkaido to Okinawa —and many different brands are produced. Koshihikari, Sasanishiki and Nihonbare are some of the best-known brands. Koshihikari and Sasanishiki are outstanding in quality and flavor and therefore are very popular.

Nutritional Value of Rice

Rice contains carbohydrates, protein, vitamins and minerals. Rice is mainly made up of carbohydrates (75%) and is therefore a significant source of energy. Starch is the main component of the carbohydrates found in rice. There are trace amounts (0.5% each) of fructose, glucose, pyranose and pentose found in the carbohydrates.

Rice contains a surprising amount of protein.

There are 7g/¼ oz of protein in 100g/3⅓ oz of rice. Compared with other grains, the amino acids are well balanced, but rice has very little lysine. By combining rice with soybean products which are rich in lysine, however, you can have a highly nutritious meal. Because rice is higher in protein than other grains, it is considered one of the best vegetable sources of protein available. In Japan, rice and *miso* soup have traditionally been served together. *Miso* is a soybean product used to make *miso* soup. Tofu (bean curd) and *aburage* (fried bean curd–tofu puff) are often added to *miso* soup, and soybeans and soybean products are also often served as side dishes. People have recently been taking a second look at these traditional combinations, which are very nutritious and healthy. Rice also contains vitamins B_1, B_2 and E. Vitamin B is contained mainly in the rice bran and vitamin E is concentrated in the rice germ. Therefore, polished rice contains fewer vitamins. However, white rice is ninety-eight percent digestible and brown rice and seventy-percent-polished rice are less easily digested.

How to Prepare Rice

In Japan, (non-glutinous) rice is generally cooked in water and served plain. This cooked rice is referred to as *gohan*. To prepare Japonica-type rice, wash it and soak in water (120% the volume of rice) for a while before cooking. Place over heat and adjust the heat as the rice cooks to achieve the best results. Traditionally, a pot (or *kama*) used only for cooking rice was used, but today most households use electric rice cookers. If you don't have a special rice cooking pot or an electric rice cooker, you can still make wonderfully moist rice with just the right amount of stickiness using a heavy bottomed pot with a tightly fitting lid.

Freshly cooked plain rice can be served with side dishes such as fish, meat and vegetables. Another way to serve rice is to flavor it. Sushi is one type of flavored rice, which is prepared by mixing flavored vinegar (a mixture of vinegar, salt and sugar) with freshly prepared rice. To prepare a variety of sushi dishes you can place ingredients atop sushi rice, mix the ingredients together with the rice, or wrap or roll the ingredients together. Sushi is indeed a special dish unique to Japan.

There are various other ways to prepare rice. *Takikomi-gohan* is cooked in water with soy sauce, salt, sugar and other ingredients. For *maze-gohan*, freshly cooked rice is mixed with flavored ingredients before serving. There is also a dish called *zosui*, in which *dashi* (Japanese soup stock) or water and other ingredients are added to cooked rice and quickly boiled. By adding more water than usual when cooking rice, you can make a dish called *okayu*, which is often served for breakfast or to people who are ill because it is extremely easy to digest. Rice is prepared in similar ways in China and Korea, although the flavors and cooking methods vary slightly.

Fried rice (*chao-fan* in Chinese) is a popular part of Chinese cuisine. Rice and other ingredients are stir-fried together in oil. Today, fried rice is often served in Japan.

In Europe and America, plain rice is not served as a staple food. Instead, it is treated like a vegetable. It is often sautéed in butter and served as a side dish or boiled and used in salads.

Glutinous rice is usually prepared after soaking in plenty of water for a long time. The glutinous rice is then drained and steamed. Steamed glutinous rice is sometimes pounded to make it even stickier and then shaped into rounds or squares. These rice cakes are called *mochi*. Freshly prepared *mochi* are warm and soft and can be lightly seasoned. Hardened *mochi* are usually grilled or boiled before serving.

Rice itself does not have a strong flavor or aroma. Therefore it can be served in a variety of

adding different flavors. It can be plain, richly flavored or spicy. Versatility is the beauty of rice.

Tips for Preparing Delicious Rice

Cooked plain rice, or *gohan*, can be served with favorite side dishes. It can also be used to make various rice dishes such as *chao-fan*, *maze-gohan* and sushi. The success of the final rice dish lies in the preparation of good plain-cooked rice. The following instructions cover how to prepare rice before it is cooked and how to adjust the heat while the rice is cooking. I hope you enjoy mastering the art of rice cooking.

How to Clean Rice

1 Rice must be cleaned before it is cooked in order to remove any remaining dirt. Fill a large bowl with water. Place the appropriate amount of rice in the bowl and wash the rice quickly. Then, quickly drain the water by placing the rice in a colander. Be sure to drain the water completely so that the rice does not absorb water which contains rice bran. (Pictures 1–2)
2 Place the rice in a bowl and add water. Stir the rice gently and drain the water. Stir the rice firmly with your fingers, pushing back and forth to remove the rice bran. Be careful not to dam-

age the grains of rice. (Picture 3)
3 Add water to the bowl again. Stir the rice five or six times with a slightly opened hand. Drain the water. Repeat this step two or three times until the rice is clean. Drain the rice in a colander. (Pictures 4-5)
4 Place the rice in a pot. Add water and let it sit for 30 minutes. For Japonica rice, add water in the amount of 120% the amount of rice (e.g. 3.6 cups of water for 3 cups of rice.) Add slightly more water for Indica rice—about 125 to 130% of the amount of rice. (Picture 6)

How to Cook Rice

1 Place a tight-fitting lid on the pot. Place over high heat and bring to a boil. Lower the heat to medium and continue cooking for 5 minutes. Turn down the heat to low and cook for 15 minutes. Turn the heat up to high for 2 seconds right before turning off the heat. Never open the lid while rice is cooking. (Pictures 7–8)
2 Remove the pot from the range and let it stand for 10 minutes to allow the rice to steam. (Picture 9)
3 Rice hardens as it cools, so be sure to mix the rice after it has stood covered for 10 minutes. First mix around the sides of the pot with a wet rice paddle (or *shamoji*). Then, mixing from the

bottom of the pot, turn the rice over and gently mix so that the rice is not in chunks.

(Pictures 10–11)

4 Until the rice is served, place a dry cloth between the pot and the lid to prevent condensation from falling on the rice. (Picture 12)

How to Measure Rice

One cup of uncooked white Japonica rice (240 cc or 190 g) makes 2.3 times its volume and weight when cooked according to the above instructions. One cup of rice makes 2.3 cups (560 cc) or about 450 g of cooked rice. The amount of rice to be prepared varies depending upon the appetite of each person, the cooking method and the combination of side dishes. As a rule of thumb, however, 3 cups of rice will serve 4 to 6 people. Adjust the amount based on this measurement.

Measurements for Automatic Rice Cooker

Rice cooker cup			American cup
1 cup	180 cc	150 g/5 oz	¾ cup
2 cups	360 cc	300 g/10 oz	1½ cups
3 cups	540 cc	450g/1 lb	2¼ cups

Raw rice	Water	
	Japonica rice + 20%	Indica rice +20 – 30%
1 cup (240 cc)	1.2 cups (288 cc) (1⅕)	1.25 cups (300 cc) – 1.3 cups (312 cc) (1¼)　　　(1⅓)
2 cups (480 cc)	2.4 cups (576 cc) (2⅖)	2.5 cups (600 cc) – 2.6 cups (624 cc) (2½)　　　(2⅗)
3 cups (720 cc)	3.6 cups (864 cc) (3⅗)	3.75 cups (900 cc) – 3.9 cups (936 cc) (3¾)　　　(4)
4 cups (960 cc)	4.8 cups (1,152 cc) (4⅘)	5 cups (1,200 cc) – 5.2 cups (1,248 cc) (5⅕)
5 cups (1,200 cc)	6 cups (1,440 cc)	6.25 cups (1,500 cc) – 6.5 cups (1,560 cc) (6¼)　　　(6½)

Metric Conversion Table

1 oz = 30 g
1 lb = 450 grams
1 teaspoon = 5 ml
1 tablespoon = 3 teaspoons = 15 ml
1 cup = 0.24 liters
1 inch = 2.5 cm

Abbreviation

tbsp: tablespoon
tsp: teaspoon

Cooking Utensils and Bowls for Japanese Rice Dishes

Ideal pots for cooking rice (Picture 1)

Using an appropriate pot is one of the most important factors in making delicious rice. When you are using an ordinary pot for cooking rice, be sure to choose a heavy-bottomed pot which conducts heat well. It is difficult to maintain a consistent temperature inside a pot with a thin bottom. This in turn causes the rice to cook unevenly, leaving some parts either under-cooked or causing the bottom to become burned. It is also very important to choose a pot which has a heavy, well-fitting lid. Cast-iron enameled pots, which are usually used to cook Western-style stews, and three- or five-layered stainless steel pots can all be used to successfully cook rice. The size and shape of the pot is also important. Since rice become 2.5 times greater in volume when cooked, choose a deep, tall pot (rather than a flat wide pot) which can accommodate four times the amount of uncooked rice.

Automatic rice cookers (Picture 2)

Rice cookers, designed specifically for preparing rice, are found in most Japanese households today. To prepare rice, simply wash the rice and place it in the rice cooker with the appropriate amount of water. After you have turned the rice cooker on, it will cook the rice and automatically switch itself off when it is done. The pot inside of the rice cooker usually has lines which indicate the appropriate amount of water to be added. By using the rice measuring cup, which usually comes with the appliance, measuring rice and water becomes very simple. Both electric rice cookers and gas rice cookers are available.

Ideal pots for preparing rice gruel and porridge (Picture 3)

Rice gruel (*okayu* in Japanese or *zhou* in Chinese), which is soft and slightly soupy, is prepared with more water than ordinary cooked rice. As the volume of rice gruel expands even more than ordinary cooked rice when cooked, you will need a large pot which can accommodate this expansion. One tip for good rice gruel is to first heat the pot of water and rice over high heat until it starts boiling, then turn down the heat to low and continue cooking slowly. For this reason, ceramic pots, which conduct heat slowly and retain heat very well, are often used in Japan and China. Rice gruel or porridge prepared in a ceramic pot remains hot for a long time after the heat has been turned off. Even after serving, this dish stays nice and warm. If a

ceramic pot is not available, you may instead use a heavy-bottomed stew pot.

Ohitsu and *handai,* wooden rice tubs for storing rice and preparing sushi rice (Picture 4)

Ohitsu and *handai* are wooden tubs for rice. An *ohitsu* is a wooden tub with a wooden lid. When the rice has finished cooking, it is placed directly from the pot into this wooden tub. The wood absorbs any excess moisture from the rice, thus preserving its fresh-cooked flavor. A *handai* is a large round and shallow wooden tub, used to prepare sushi rice. Freshly cooked rice is placed in the wooden tub. A vinegar mixture is added to the rice and mixed well. The shape of the *handai* allows for both the vinegar mixture to be easily incorporated with the rice, and for the rice to cool down quickly as it is spread out across a wide area. A wooden rice paddle, called *shamoji,* is used to mix and serve the rice. The rice paddle should be moistened beforehand to prevent the rice from sticking.

Bowls for serving rice . (Picture 5)

In Japan, rice is usually served in a bowl. In Europe and America, people use forks and knives to dine, however in many Asian countries including Japan, chopsticks are used. Serving rice in a bowl makes it easier to eat with chopsticks and keeps the rice warm for a longer time.

When plain rice is to be eaten with other side dishes, it is usually served in individual rice bowls with diameters of roughly 10 cm. When there is a main dish served on top of rice (*don-buri* style) or mixed with rice (*maze-gohan* style), slightly larger bowls are used for each individual serving. There are ceramic rice bowls as well as lacquered ones.

Lunch boxes (*obento bako*) (Picture 6)

In Japan, there is a wide variety of lunch boxes available. There are lunch boxes which are designed to be brought along on picnics, to school and to the office. There are also lunch boxes which are designed for serving more formal meals for visitors at home. Lunch boxes to be used outside of the home are designed to be simple, but practical. They are made of wood, bamboo, plastic, or alumite (a type of corrosion-resistant aluminum), and they come in a variety of shapes such as rectangular, rectangular with rounded corners, and round. There are also lunch boxes which have dividers inside to separate the rice from the other foods. Lunch boxes made of lacquered wood and decorated with sophisticated Japanese designs are usually used for serving meals to visitors at home. The traditional Japanese lunch box, or *shokado,* is also designed for use in the home. It is a rectangular or square box with cross-dividers. There are other types of lunch boxes which are designed with two or three different levels and which are available in rectangular, round and half-moon shapes. In all cases, lunch boxes are designed to hold rice and other foods in one container.

Takikomi Gohan and Pilaf

Takikomi gohan is a type of Japanese rice dish. Various ingredients such as vegetables, seafood and chicken are combined with *dashi* (Japanese soup stock), and other seasonings. The ingredients are then cooked together with the rice.

Rice Flavored with Chicken and Vegetables (*Kayaku gohan*)

Kayaku gohan uses seven different ingredients, including chicken and burdock root.

Makes 4 servings
2 rice cooker cups of rice
Seasoning Mix A:
   2 tablespoons light soy sauce
   3 tablespoons saké
   ⅓ teaspoon salt
150 g/5 oz skinless chicken breast
1 piece tofu puff (*aburage*)
2 dried *shiitake* mushrooms
½ burdock root (60 g/2 oz)
⅓ carrot (40 g/1⅓ oz)
¼ *konnyaku* cake
20 g/⅔ oz snow peas

1 About 30 minutes to an hour before cooking, wash the rice well and drain in a colander.
2 Cut the chicken breast in half lengthwise (making it twice as thin) and then slice into 3 cm/1 inch long pieces. Place the tofu puff in a colander and pour boiling water over it to remove excess oil. Cut the piece lengthwise and then cut into 3 cm/1 inch slices. Soak the dried *shiitake* mushrooms in water until soft. Reserve the liquid. Remove and discard the stems and cut into thin pieces.
3 Peel the burdock root and carrot. Cut them crosswise into thin shavings, as if sharpening a pencil. Soak the burdock root shavings in a bowl of water with a little rice vinegar added for 5 minutes to remove the harshness. Thinly slice *konnyaku* into 3 cm/1 inch lengths.
4 Add the rice and Seasoning Mix A to the rice cooker. Add the reserved *shiitake* liquid and water if needed to fill to the two-cup measuring line. Add the rest of the ingredients and mix well. Switch on the rice cooker. After the rice has finished cooking, let stand for 12–13 minutes longer. Mix well. (Pictures 1–3)
5 Evenly divide the rice into four individual serving bowls and garnish with sliced snow peas before serving.

Green Peas and Rice (*Aomame gohan*)

The flavor and scent of the green peas permeates this wonderfully seasoned rice.

Makes 4 servings
2 rice cooker cups of rice
Seasoning Mix A:
  1 tablespoon saké
  1 teaspoon salt
200 g/7 oz green peas (freshly shelled)
150 g/5 oz skinless chicken breast
Seasoning Mix B:
  1 teaspoon saké
  Dash of salt

1 About 30 minutes to an hour before cooking, wash the rice well and drain in a colander.
2 Cut the chicken breast into 1 cm/½ inch cubes and season with Seasoning Mix B.
3 Add the rice and Seasoning Mix A to the rice cooker. Add water to fill to the two-cup measuring line. Add the chicken and green peas and mix well. Let stand for 20–30 minutes before cooking. Mix again briefly, making sure that the mixture is evenly distributed and that all the pieces are under water. Then switch on the rice cooker. After the rice has finished cooking, let it sit for 10–15 minutes. Then mix well.

* If you want the green peas to retain their bright color, boil them in salted water for 3–5 minutes and place in water to cool. Then add the green peas to the rice cooker immediately after the rice has finished cooking.

Sea Bream and Rice (*Tai gohan*)

Cook the sea bream pieces whole with rice and then break into pieces.

Makes 4 servings
2 rice cooker cups of rice
10 cm/4 inch piece of sea kelp (*konbu*)
Seasoning Mix A:
  2 tablespoons saké
  ½ tablespoon soy sauce
  1 teaspoon salt
4 pieces sea bream (250 g/8⅓ oz)
Seasoning Mix B:
  1 tablespoon saké
  1 teaspoon salt
Leaves from a *kinome*

1 About 1 hour before cooking, wash the rice well and drain in a colander. Thirty minutes before cooking, place rice in the rice cooker and add water to just under the two-cup level. Wipe the piece of sea kelp clean and add it to the rice cooker.

2 Season the sea bream with Seasoning Mix B.

3 Remove the sea kelp from the rice cooker. Add Seasoning Mix A and mix well. Drain the sea bream well and place the pieces on the rice, skin side facing up. Switch on the rice cooker.

4 When the rice has finished cooking, allow it to stand for 12 minutes. Then, remove the pieces of sea bream from the rice cooker. Remove the small bones and break the pieces apart. Place the sea bream back in the rice cooker and mix well.

5 Divide the rice into four individual serving bowls. Slap the *kinome* between your palms to release their flavors, and then use as a garnish.

Chestnuts and Rice (*Kuri gohan*)

This dish, seasoned with a touch of salt, is a colorful mix of ingredients.

Makes 4 servings
2 rice cooker cups of rice
Seasoning Mix A:
   2 tablespoons saké
   1 teaspoon salt
2⅓ cups *kobu dashi* stock, sea kelp based
20 small chestnuts
8 prawns (*taisho ebi*)
Seasoning Mix B:
   ½ tablespoon saké
   Dash of salt
20 g/⅔ oz green beans

1 Soak the chestnuts in salted water for 12 hours. When the peels have softened, make a slit in each and remove. Make sure that you also remove the very thin skin beneath the peel. Soak the peeled chestnuts in water until ready to use.
2 About 30 minutes to an hour before cooking, wash the rice well and drain in a colander.

3 Shell and devein the prawns and cut each into 2–3 pieces. Rub with Seasoning Mix B.
4 Boil the green beans until they turn bright green. Let cool in a bowl of water and cut into 1 cm/½ inch pieces.
5 Add the rice and Seasoning Mix A to the rice cooker. Add the *kobu dashi* stock to fill to just under the two-cup measuring line. Add the chestnuts and well-drained prawns and mix well, making sure that the mixture is evenly distributed and that all ingredients are under water. Then switch on the rice cooker. After the rice has finished cooking, add the green beans and let the rice sit for 15–20 minutes. Then mix well.

Note: If you are using large chestnuts, 15–16 chestnuts will be enough for this recipe. If this is the case, cut the chestnuts in half.

For variation, you can use roasted chestnuts. To roast the chestnuts, peel off part of the skin and place on a grill. Roast until the skin pops.

Matsutake Mushrooms and Rice (*Matsutake gohan*)

As the rice cooks, the wonderful smell of *matsutake* mushrooms fills the room. You ought to try this dish at least once, when these mushrooms are in season.

Makes 4 servings
2 rice cooker cups of rice
⅓ teaspoon salt
2 *matsutake* mushrooms (100 g/3⅓ oz) or
 shiitake mushrooms
Seasoning A:
 2 tablespoons saké
 2 tablespoons soy sauce
1 piece tofu puff (*aburage*)
2 *kabosu* (Japanese lime-like citrus)

1 About 30 minutes to an hour before cooking, wash the rice well and drain in a colander.
2 Gently scrape the dirt from the stems of the *matsutake* mushrooms. Quickly wash in lightly salted water. Cut crosswise into 2–3 cm/1 inch lengths. Then thinly slice each piece lengthwise. Soak the *matsutake* mushroom slices in Seasoning Mix A for 20–30 minutes.
3 Place the tofu puff in a colander and pour boiling water over it to remove excess oil. Cut the piece lengthwise and then cut into thin strips.
4 Add the rice, liquid from the *matsutake* mushrooms and salt to the rice cooker. Add water to fill to just under the two-cup measuring line. Add the *matsutake* mushrooms and tofu puff and mix well, making sure that the mixture is evenly distributed and that all the ingredients are under water. Then switch on the rice cooker. After the rice has finished cooking, let it sit for 10–15 minutes. Then mix well before serving.
5 Place the rice in a serving bowl and set *kabosu* (cut in half) alongside the rice. Complement with a few different kinds of pickles at the side of the bowl.

Oysters and Rice (*Kaki gohan*)

If you cook the oysters with the rice, they will shrink too much, so add them when the rice has finished cooking.

Makes 4 servings
2 rice cooker cups of rice
350 g/12 oz shelled oysters
Cooking Liquid:
   1⅓ tablespoons saké
   1 tablespoon soy sauce
   ⅓ teaspoon salt
   ⅔ cup water
Small piece fresh ginger root
1 *kabosu* (Japanese lime-like citrus)
A small piece toasted *nori* seaweed (*yaki nori*)

1 About 30 minutes to an hour before cooking, wash the rice well and drain in a colander.
2 Place the oysters in a colander and then place the colander in a bowl of salted water. Shake the colander to wash the oysters and then drain well.
3 Add the ingredients for the Cooking Liquid to a shallow pot and bring to a boil. Add the oysters and stir gently. When the oysters puff up, pour the oysters and sauce into a colander over a bowl to separate the oysters from the sauce.
4 Thinly slice the ginger into strips.
5 Add the rice and enough sauce from the oysters to the rice cooker to fill to the two-cup measuring line. Let stand for 20–30 minutes, then switch on the rice cooker. After the rice has finished cooking, top it with the oysters and ginger and let it sit for 10–15 minutes. Then mix well.
6 Tear *nori* into small pieces. Cut *kabosu* into four wedges. Divide the rice into four individual serving bowls. Sprinkle the *nori* over the rice. Before eating, squeeze *kabosu* over the rice.

Japanese Pumpkin and Rice (*Kabocha gohan*)

Salty bacon and sweet pumpkin are well suited for each other.

Makes 4 servings
2 rice cooker cups of rice
½ teaspoon salt
300 g/10 oz *kabocha* (Japanese pumpkin)
4 slices bacon (about 60 g/2 oz)
Minced parsley

1 About 30 minutes to an hour before cooking, wash the rice well and drain in a colander.
2 Remove the *kabocha* seeds with a spoon and peel small parts of the skin away, for a mottled appearance. Cut the *kabocha* into about 1.5 cm/⅔ inch cubes.
3 Cut the slices of bacon into 1.5 cm/⅔ inch-wide pieces. Quickly boil to remove excess fat.
4 Add the rice and the salt to the rice cooker. Add water to fill to the two-cup measuring line. Add the *kabocha* and bacon and mix well. Let stand for 20–30 minutes before cooking. Mix roughly, making sure that the mixture is evenly distributed and the ingredients are under water. Then switch on the rice cooker. After the rice has finished cooking, let it sit for 10–15 minutes. Then mix well. Evenly divide into four individual serving bowls and sprinkle with minced parsley.

Note: For variation, substitute sweet potato (*satsumaimo*) for *kabocha*.

Seafood Pilaf

This dish makes the most of the vibrant color and piquant aroma of saffron. Stir-fry the ingredients before adding them to the rice.

Makes 4 servings

2 rice cooker cups of rice
Ingredients A:
  ½ teaspoon saffron threads or
    2 tablespoons curry powder
  1 cup water
  ⅓ cup white wine
1 small squid, whole
12 prawns
8 mussels
⅓ onion
1 clove garlic
1 tablespoon salad oil
1 teaspoon salt
Dash of pepper
12 stuffed olives
Few sprigs of Italian parsley
½ lemon

1 About 30 minutes to an hour before cooking, wash the rice well and drain in a colander.

2 Combine Ingredients A in a small pot and heat until just before boiling. (Picture 1)

3 Skin the sac part of the squid and cut into 1 cm/½ inch-wide rings. Separate the tentacles from the innards and bony mouth. Remove the suckers from the tentacles and peel off the skin. Shell the prawns, being careful not to remove the section closest to the tail; devein. Scrub the outside of the mussels' shells carefully.

4 Mince the onion and garlic.

5 Heat a frying pan and add salad oil. Sauté the onion and garlic until the onion becomes translucent. Add the squid, prawns and mussels and stir-fry quickly. Season with salt and pepper. (Picture 2)

6 Place rice in the rice cooker. Add the saffron, water and wine mixture and (if necessary) more water to reach the two-cup level. Add the stir-fried seafood and liquid from the frying pan to the rice cooker and cook. When the rice has finished cooking, allow it to sit for 10–15 minutes. (Picture 3)

7 Place the rice in individual serving dishes. Garnish with stuffed olives, Italian parsley and lemon wedges.

Curry Pilaf with Sausage (*Soseji no kare pirafu*)

A quick rice dish flavored with curry and sausage.

Makes 6 servings
3 cups uncooked rice
Soup Stock:
  2 bouillon cubes
  3 cups hot water
6 sausages
1 small onion
2 sweet red peppers
6 mushrooms
1 tablespoon salad oil
1½ tablespoons butter
1 tablespoon curry powder
Seasoning Mix B:
  1 teaspoon salt
  Dash of pepper
  1 tablespoon white wine

1 Wash the rice 30 minutes before cooking and drain in a colander.
2 To make the soup stock, dissolve the bouillon cubes in hot water.
3 Cut the sausage diagonally into 5 mm/¼ inch slices.
4 Dice the onion and sweet red peppers into 1 cm/½ inch square pieces. Remove the stems from the mushrooms and slice diagonally into 5 mm/¼ inch slices.
5 Heat the salad oil in a heavy pot. Quickly stir-fry the sausage, onion, sweet red peppers and mushrooms.
6 Add the butter and rice and stir-fry for a short time longer. Add the curry powder and continue to stir-fry.
7 Add the soup and Seasoning Mix B and mix. Cover and bring to a boil. Turn down the heat to medium and cook for 5 minutes. Reduce the heat to low and continue cooking for 15 minutes. Turn the heat off and let stand for 10 minutes. Mix the rice before serving.

Korean-Style Pilaf with Beef and Soybean Sprouts
(*Gyuniku to moyashi no kankokufu pirafu*)

The aroma of garlic, chives and sesame seeds brings out the wonderful flavors of this dish.

Makes 6 servings
3 cups uncooked rice
200 g/7 oz thinly sliced beef
Seasoning Mix:
   1 teaspoon soy sauce
   1 teaspoon saké
200 g/7 oz soybean sprouts
1 clove garlic
½ green onion
3 tablespoons sesame oil
Cooking Liquid:
   1½ tablespoons soy sauce
   1 tablespoon saké
   1 teaspoon salt
   Dash of pepper
   3⅔ cups water
1–2 tablespoons toasted white sesame seeds
2 scallion stalks, minced
1–2 hot chilli peppers, finely sliced

1 Wash the rice 30 minutes before cooking and drain in a colander.
2 Cut the beef into 1 cm/½ inch strips. Season with Seasoning Mix.
3 Wash the soybean sprouts and drain well. Cut them in half if they are long.
4 Mince the garlic and green onions.
5 Heat the sesame oil in a heavy pot. Quickly stir-fry the garlic and green onions. When their aroma is released, add the beef and stir-fry until brown. Add the rice and continue to stir-fry for a short time longer.
6 Add the soybean sprouts and Cooking Liquid. Quickly mix, cover the pot and bring to a boil. When it starts to boil, lower the heat to medium and cook for 5 minutes. Reduce the heat to low and continue to cook for another 15 minutes. Turn off the heat and let stand for 10 minutes before serving.
7 Arrange of pilaf on each plate and sprinkle with minced scallions and hot chilli peppers.

Red Beans and Rice (*Okowa*)

Using a microwave oven makes preparing this dish easier than the traditional method of steaming.

Makes 4 servings
2 cups glutinous rice
40 g/1⅓ oz dried adzuki beans (*sasage*)
  *Reserve the bean cooking liquid and combine with water to make 1⅗ cup of liquid for cooking the rice.
Salt (less than a dash)
1½ tablespoons sesame-salt (*gomashio*)

1 To boil the beans: Add washed beans and 2 cups of water to a pot and bring to a boil. Stir the beans by scooping them out of the water with a slotted spoon and then returning them to the pot. Continue cooking and "stirring" in this way for 5–6 minutes. (When beans are exposed to the air while they are cooking their color

brightens.) Turn off the heat, and let stand for 5–6 minutes. Then place the beans in a colander, making sure to reserve the cooking liquid.

2 Put beans back in the pot, add 2 cups of water and bring to a boil. Then quickly reduce the heat to low and continue cooking until the beans become soft. It is important to avoid breaking the beans' delicate skin. Drain in a colander and sprinkle with a tiny bit of salt.

3 Wash the glutinous rice and place in a deep microwave-safe bowl (preferable with a lid). Combine the reserved cooking liquid with water to make 1⅗ cup of water. Add this mixture to the rice and let stand for 30 minutes.

4 Add the beans to the rice and cover. (If there is no lid, use plastic wrap). Microwave at 500W for 10 minutes. Quickly mix from the bottom, and cover again. Continue to cook in the microwave for 3–4 minutes. When the rice is done cooking, let it stand for an additional 10 minutes.

5 Place the rice in a serving bowl and sprinkle with sesame salt before serving.

*When microwaving at 600W, shorten the cooking time by 20%. If microwaving at 400W, extend the cooking time by 20%.

Chinese-Style Cooked Glutinous Rice (*Chuka okowa*)

Roasted pork, dried shrimp, and chestnuts cooked in a microwave oven with rice.

Makes 4 servings
2 cups glutinous rice
Seasoning Mix A:
   1½ cups soup (made from combining chicken
     soup stock with the soaking liquid from the
     dried shrimp)
   2 tablespoons saké
   1 tablespoon soy sauce
   1 teaspoon sugar
   ½ teaspoon salt
100 g/3⅓ oz Chinese roasted pork
1 tablespoon dried shrimp
2 dried *shiitake* mushrooms
50 g/2 oz boiled bamboo shoots
⅓ green onion
4 chestnuts cooked in sweet sauce
1 teaspoon sesame oil
1 teaspoon salad oil
Fresh coriander, for garnish

1 To reconstitute the dried shrimp, soak them in warm water. (This water will later be used to make soup.) Soak the dried *shiitake* mushrooms. Remove and discard the stems and dice into 7–8 mm/¼ inch cubes. Cut the broiled pork and bamboo shoots into 7–8 mm/¼ inch cubes. Cut the green onion into 8 mm/¼ inch- wide rounds.
2 Cut each sweetened chestnut into 3–4 pieces. (Picture 1)
3 Wash the glutinous rice and place in a deep microwave safe bowl (preferably with its own lid). Add Seasoning Mix A and let stand for 10–15 minutes. (Picture 2)
4 Add the shrimp, *shiitake*, pork, bamboo shoots and green onions to the rice. Add the sesame oil and salad oil and mix well. Cover. (If there is no lid, use plastic wrap). Microwave at 500W for 10 minutes. Quickly mix from the bottom, add the chestnuts, and cover again. Continue to microwave for 4–5 minutes. When the rice is done cooking, let it stand for an additional 10 minutes. Mix very well. Place in a serving dish. Garnish with coriander. (Pictures 3–6)

Small *Aemono* Dishes and *Ohitashi*

Refreshing Japanese-style salads go very well with *takikomi gohan*.
The vegetables are simply boiled and dressed with
a variety of dressings. Enjoy!

Enoki Mushrooms and *Daikon* Sprouts Cooked in Broth
(*Enokidake to kaiwarena no nibitashi*)

Makes 4 servings
1 bunch *enoki* mushrooms, 200 g/7½ oz *daikon* sprouts
Cooking Broth: ⅔ cup *dashi* stock, 1½ tbsp soy sauce, ½ tbsp *mirin*

1 Stem and separate the *enoki* mushrooms. Cut off the bottom part of the *daikon* sprouts.
2 Mix the Cooking Broth and bring to a boil. Add the *enoki* mushrooms and *daikon* sprouts. Stir gently and cook for another 30 seconds.

Chinese Scallions Tossed with Seaweed
(*Nira no nori ae*)

Makes 4 servings
1 bunch Chinese scallions
1 sheet toasted *nori* seaweed (*yaki-nori*)
Mixture A: 2 tbsp *dashi* stock, 2 tbsp soy sauce

1 Cut scallions into 3 cm/1¼ inch lengths. Quickly boil in a pot of water, while stirring. Place in a colander and pour water over the scallions to cool them down.
2 Toss the scallions with Mixture A. Tear *nori* seaweed into small pieces and mix in well with the scallions.

Komatsuna in Mustard Sauce
(*Komatsuna no karashi ae*)

Makes 4 servings
1 bunch *komatsuna*
Dressing: ½ tbsp Japanese hot mustard (*wagarashi*), 1 tbsp soy sauce, 1 tbsp *mirin*

1 Boil 1 bunch of *komatsuna* until it turns bright green. Plunge into water to cool. Remove and squeeze out excess water. Cut into 5 cm/2 inch lengths.
2 Dress the *komatsuna* with Dressing.

Asparagus in *Miso* Mayonnaise Dressing
(*Asuparagasu no miso mayoneizu ae*)

Makes 4 servings
6 stalks asparagus
Dressing: 3 tbsp mayonnaise, 1 tbsp *miso*

1 Snap off the tough part of the stems of asparagus. Boil the asparagus just until it turns bright green. Drain in a colander and cut into 3–4 cm/1½ inch lengths.
2 Divide the asparagus into four small individual serving dishes. Mix Dressing well and place atop the asparagus.

Cabbage in Sesame Soy Sauce Dressing
(*Kyabetsu no gomajoyu ae*)

Makes 4 servings
¼ head cabbage, 2 tbsp toasted white sesame seeds
Sesame Dressing: 1 tbsp soy sauce, 1 tbsp *dashi* stock, 1 tsp sesame oil, dash of salt

1 Chop cabbage into bite-sized pieces. Quickly boil and drain in a colander. Spread out the leaves to allow the cabbage to cool.
2 Dress the cabbage with Sesame Dressing.
3 Divide the cabbage into four small individual serving dishes. Sprinkle with half-ground toasted white sesame seeds.

Chao-fan and *Maze-gohan*

Chao-fan (*chahan* in Japanese) is a simple Chinese dish. Rice and other ingredients are stir-fried in a Chinese wok. *Maze gohan* is a Japanese-style dish in which ingredients such as meat and vegetables are prepared beforehand and then mixed together with freshly prepared rice.

Five-Flavored Fried Rice (*Gomoku chahan*)

With chopped ham and vegetables, this dish is savory and nutritious.

Makes 4 servings

2 rice cooker cups of rice, cooked
2 eggs
  ¼ teaspoon salt
70 g/2½ oz piece ham
2 large dried *shiitake* mushrooms
50 g/2 oz boiled bamboo shoots
1 green onion
2 tablespoons frozen green peas
4 tablespoons salad oil
  1¾ teaspoon salt
Dash of pepper
1 tablespoon soy sauce

1 Soak the dried *shiitake* mushrooms to reconstitute. Remove and discard the stems. Dice the ham and boiled bamboo shoots into 5 mm/¼ inch cubes.

2 Cut the green onion lengthwise into 4–6 pieces. Then cut into 5 mm/¼ inch pieces. Place the green peas into a colander and pour boiling water over them.

3 Beat the egg and add salt.

4 Heat a Chinese wok and add half of the salad oil. Pour in the beaten egg. When the egg starts to cook, roughly scramble until half cooked. Set aside. (Picture 1)

5 Add the remaining salad oil to the wok. Quickly sauté the *shiitake*, ham and bamboo shoots over high heat. Sprinkle ¼ teaspoon of salt over the mixture.

6 Add green onions and quickly sauté. Then add cooked rice and continue to sauté over medium heat. (Picture 2)

7 Add the egg, breaking it into small pieces as you proceed. Add the green peas. Continue mixing until all the ingredients are evenly distributed. Season with salt and pepper. Lastly, carefully add the soy sauce around the sides of the wok so that it sizzles and burns slightly before it reaches the rice. Continue mixing and cook for a short time longer. (Picture 3)

Prawns and Pineapple Fried Rice (*Ebi to painappuru no chahan*)

The refreshing flavor of this dish comes from the pineapple's combination of tart and sweet.

Makes 4 servings
2 rice cooker cups of rice, cooked
Seasoning Mix A:
   1¼ teaspoons salt
   Dash of pepper
8 prawns
Seasoning Mix B:
   ½ teaspoon salt
   2 teaspoons saké
   2 teaspoons *katakuriko* or cornstarch
½ fresh pineapple (200 g/7 oz)
20 g/⅔ oz string beans
2 eggs
   ¼ teaspoon salt
   Dash of pepper
6 tablespoons salad oil

1 Shell and devein the prawns. Cut in half and coat with Seasoning Mix B.
2 Peel the pineapple and slice into 1 cm/½ inch slices. Remove and discard the core. Chop into small pieces.
3 Quickly boil the string beans, and cut diagonally into 1 cm/½ inch pieces.
4 Mix cooked rice with Seasoning Mix A.
5 Beat the eggs and season with salt and pepper.
6 Heat a frying pan and add 2 tablespoons of the salad oil. Add the beaten eggs. When the eggs start to bubble, roughly scramble until half cooked and then set aside.
7 Reheat the pan and add 1 tablespoon of salad oil. Stir-fry the prawns over high heat and then set aside.
8 Add the remaining 3 tablespoons of salad oil to the heated wok. Stir-fry the rice over medium heat. Mix the egg in quickly, breaking them up into smaller pieces as you proceed. Add the prawns, pineapple and green beans and continue sautéing for 1–2 minutes.

Crab and Lettuce Fried Rice (*Kani to retasu no chahan*)

Fresh lettuce adds crispness to this dish.

Makes 4 servings
2 rice cooker cups of rice, cooked
Seasoning Mix A:
   1¾ teaspoons salt
   Dash of pepper
200 g/7 oz crab meat
4 lettuce leaves
1 green onion
½ cup green soybeans, removed from
  their pods (*edamame*)
4 tablespoons salad oil

1 Mix Seasoning Mix A with warm rice.
2 Remove any soft bones (cartilage) from the crab meat.
3 Cut the lettuce into 3–4 cm/1⅔ inch squares. Mince the green onion. Peel the thin skin from the soybeans.
4 Heat a Chinese wok and add the salad oil. Sauté the minced green onion over medium heat. Add the cooked rice and stir-fry until the rice is no longer sticky.
5 Add the crab meat and soybeans and continue to stir-fry for 1–2 minutes. Quickly mix in the lettuce, being careful not to overcook it.

Special Egg Fried Rice
(*Tamago chahan*)

Season the rice, coat with egg and then stir-fry.

Makes 4 servings
2 rice cooker cups of rice, cooked
1½ teaspoons salt
Dash of pepper
4 eggs, beaten
120 g/4 oz sliced ham
½ thin green onion
6 tablespoons salad oil
Few sprigs of Italian parsley

1 Cut the ham into 5 mm/¼ inch squares. Thinly slice the green onion.
2 Place cooked rice into a bowl and season with salt and pepper. Add the beaten eggs and mix very well. (Picture 1)
3 Heat a frying pan and add half of the salad oil and half the rice. Stir-fry by mixing from the bottom of the wok until the rice is no longer sticky and the egg is completely cooked.
(Pictures 2–3)
4 Add half of the ham and green onions. Quickly mix and cook until the fragrance of the green onion is released. Prepare the other half of the ingredients in the same way. Divide the fried rice among the serving plates and garnish with sprigs of Italian parsley. (Pictures 4–5)

Jade Fried Rice (*Hisui chahan*)

Chinese greens add beauty and elegance to this dish.

Makes 4 servings
2 rice cooker cups of rice, cooked
300 g/10 oz Chinese greens (*ching-kêng-cai*)
   ½ teaspoon salt
8 prawns (black tiger)
½ teaspoon salt
1 teaspoon saké
4 tablespoons salad oil
1 teaspoon salt
Dash of pepper

1 Mince the *ching-kêng-cai*. Sprinkle with salt and rub lightly. Set aside. When the water is released from the *ching-kêng-cai*, place in cheesecloth and gently squeeze.

2 Shell and devein the prawns and cut into 1 cm/½ inch pieces. Rub with salt and toss with saké.

3 Heat a frying pan and add salad oil. Stir-fry the *ching-kêng-cai* over high heat, breaking up the pieces as you go. Add the prawns and continue to stir-fry until they turn pink.

4 Add cooked rice to the pan and reduce the heat to medium. Stir-fry until the rice is no longer sticky. Season with salt and pepper and continue cooking for 1–2 minutes.

Fried Rice with Pickled Chinese Mustard Greens and Ground Meat
(*Takana to hikiniku no chahan*)

The key to this dish lies in the strong salty flavor of the pickles.

Makes 4 servings

2 rice cooker cups of rice, cooked
150 g/5 oz ground pork
150 g/5 oz pickled Chinese mustard greens
   (pickled *takana*; *takana-zuke*)
1 tablespoon toasted white sesame seeds
2 tablespoons salad oil
1 tablespoon sesame oil
1 teaspoon brown bean paste (*tou-pan-jang*)
Dash of salt
½ tablespoon soy sauce

1 Wash *takana-zuke* thoroughly and squeeze to remove excess water. Mince.

2 Heat a frying pan, then add salad and sesame oils. Stir-fry the ground pork until it no longer sticks together. Add the *tou-pan-jiang* and stir-fry until its aroma is released.

3 Add cooked rice and lower the heat to medium. Stir-fry until the rice no longer sticks together.

4 Add the *takana-zuke* and sesame seeds and stir-fry quickly. Season with a tiny bit of salt and soy sauce. You need not add much salt since the pickles are already quite salty.

Note: You may use other types of pickled greens, such as *nozawana-zuke*.

Beef and Watercress Fried Rice (*Gyuniku to kureson no chahan*)

The addition of walnuts and curry powder makes this dish similar to dry curry.

Makes 4 servings
2 rice cooker cups of rice, cooked
200 g/7 oz thinly sliced or finely cut beef
  ⅛ teaspoon salt
  Dash of pepper
1 bunch watercress
50 g/2 oz shelled walnuts
½ green onion
1 piece ginger
1 clove garlic
3 tablespoons salad oil
1 tablespoon curry powder
1 teaspoon salt
Dash of pepper

1 Cut the beef into 1 cm/½ inch pieces. Season with salt and pepper. Separate the stems from the leaves of the watercress. Cut the stems into 1 cm/½ inch lengths. Roughly chop the walnuts.

2 Mince the green onion, ginger and garlic.

3 Heat a Chinese wok and add salad oil. Stir-fry the minced green onion, ginger and garlic until their aroma is released. Add the beef and stir-fry over high heat until cooked. Add the watercress stems and walnuts and continue cooking for 20–30 seconds. Mix in the curry powder and stir-fry for 1–2 minutes.

4 Add cooked rice and reduce heat to medium. Continue to stir-fry until the rice no longer sticks together. Season with salt and pepper. Mix in the watercress leaves and cook for 20–30 seconds.

Rice Mixed with Stir-Fried Pork and *Hijiki*
(*Butaniku to hijiki itame no maze-gohan*)

This healthy dish, chock-full of calcium and fiber, is gaining popularity.

Makes 4 servings
2 rice cooker cups of rice, cooked
100 g/3⅓ oz pork
   1 teaspoon saké
   1 teaspoon soy sauce
20 g/⅔ oz dried *hijiki* seaweed, soaked in water
   8–10 minutes. Drain and rinse to remove sand.
10 g/⅓ oz dried *daikon*, soak in water for 10–15
   minutes. Drain and rinse well. Squeeze out.
1½ tablespoons sesame oil
Seasoning Mix A:
   1 tablespoon saké
   2½ tablespoons soy sauce
   2 tablespoons *mirin*
Scrambled Egg
   1 egg
   ⅛ teaspoon salt
   ½ tablespoon salad oil
20 g/⅔ oz snow peas

1 Cut *hijiki* into short pieces. Cut dried *daikon* into shorter pieces.

2 Cut the pork into 5 mm/¼ inch pieces. Season with saké and soy sauce.

3 Heat a frying pan and add sesame oil. Stir-fry the pork until well-cooked. Add the *hijiki* and dried *daikon* (*kiriboshi-daikon*) and continue to stir-fry. Add Seasoning Mix A. Continue to stir-fry until the liquid is nearly gone.

4 To make the scrambled egg, beat the egg and mix in the salt. Heat a small pan and add the oil. Pour in the egg and stir using chopsticks. Continue to cook until well-scrambled.

5 Boil the snow peas until they turn bright green and thinly slice at a diagonal.

6 About 10 minutes after the rice has finished cooking, mix the rice well from the bottom. Then add the pork and *hijiki* mixture and the snow peas to the freshly cooked rice and continue to mix. Divide the rice mixture into four individual serving bowls and place a quarter of the scrambled egg in the center of each serving.

Rice Mixed with Bacon and Lotus Root
(*Beikon to renkon itame no maze-gohan*)

You don't need to add any oil to this dish because of the bacon fat.

Makes 4 servings
2 rice cooker cups of rice, cooked
5 slices bacon (about 100 g/3⅓ oz)
1 section lotus root (150 g/5 oz)
1 bunch watercress
1 teaspoon salt
Dash of pepper
1/10 teaspoon coarsely ground pepper

1 Peel the lotus root and slice into rounds or half-moons and soak in vinegared water (1 tablespoon rice vinegar to 3 cups water) for 10 minutes. Cut the bacon into 1 cm/½ inch pieces. Pinch off the leaves of the watercress and cut the stems into 2 cm/1 inch lengths.

2 Heat a frying pan and add the bacon. Fry until the fat has been cooked out of the bacon and the bacon becomes crispy. Add lotus root and watercress stems. Stir-fry until the lotus roots become somewhat transparent. Season with salt and pepper and remove from the heat.
3 About 10 minutes after the rice has finished cooking, mix the rice well from the bottom. Then add the bacon and lotus root mixture to the freshly cooked rice and mix well. Place the rice mixture in four individual serving dishes. Garnish with the watercress leaves and sprinkle the coarsely ground pepper over each serving.

Rice Mixed with Scrambled Egg and Tuna
(*Tsuna iritamago no maze-gohan*)

For a spicier flavor, add some spicy Chinese *miso* (*dou-ban-jiang*) before serving.

Makes 4 servings
2 rice cooker cups of rice, cooked
6 eggs
Seasoning Mix A:
    ¼ teaspoon salt
    ½ tablespoon sugar
    ½ teaspoon rice vinegar
1 can tuna (about 190 g/6⅓ oz), drained
100 g/3⅓ oz green garlic sprouts (*suan-tai*)
2 tablespoons salad oil
1½ teaspoons salt
Dash of pepper
Chinese brown soybean paste (*dou-ban-jiang*)
    optional

1 Break the tuna into small pieces. Cut the garlic stems into 1 cm/½ inch lengths.

2 Beat the eggs and mix in Seasoning Mix A. Add the tuna and mix quickly.

3 Heat a large frying pan or a heavy pot. Add salad oil and sauté the garlic sprouts until they turn bright green. Pour the beaten egg mixture into the pan and stir with chopsticks, quickly at first. Towards the end of cooking, break the scrambled eggs into small pieces.

4 About 10 minutes after the rice has finished cooking, mix well from the bottom. Then mix the scrambled egg mixture into the freshly cooked rice. Season with salt and pepper and mix well.

Small Soups

Soup goes very well with *chao-fan*.
This section features five lightly flavored soups.

Tomato and Egg Flower Soup
(*Tomato no kakitama supu*)

Makes 4 servings
2 tbsp dried shrimp, 5½ cups warm water, ½ onion, 2 tomatoes, 2 eggs, 3 tbsp salad oil, 5½ cups water, 1¼ tsp salt, dash of pepper

1 Soak dried shrimp in warm water to reconstitute. Remove the shells from the shrimp and place shrimp back in the warm water.
2 Thinly slice onion. Peel tomatoes. Cut each tomato into eight wedges and remove seeds.
3 Sauté onion and tomatoes in salad oil. Add the shrimp and water in which they have been soaking. Season with salt and pepper. Bring to a boil. Pour two beaten eggs into boiling soup to make egg flowers.

Salad Greens and
Wakame Seaweed Soup
(*Sarada-na to wakame no supu*)

Makes 4 servings
10 g/⅔ oz salted *wakame* seaweed, 4 salad green leaves
Cooking Broth: 4 cups chicken stock, ¾ tsp salt, 1 tsp soy sauce, 1 tsp sesame oil

1 Wash *wakame* seaweed and chop into small bite-sized pieces. Cut salad greens into 1 cm/½ inch-wide strips.
2 Mix Cooking Broth in a pot. Bring to a boil. Add *wakame* seaweed and boil again.
3 Place salad greens in small soup bowls and ladle hot soup over the greens.

Quail Egg Soup (*Uzura tamago supu*)

Makes 4 servings
8 quail eggs, 4–5 sprigs *mitsuba* trefoil
Cooking Broth: 4 cups chicken stock, 1¼ tsp salt, 2 tsp soy sauce, dash of pepper

1 Combine Cooking Broth in a pot and bring to a boil.
2 Gently break 2 eggs into each soup bowl and add a small amount of roughly chopped trefoil. Ladle boiling soup from the edge of the soup bowl. The eggs will quickly become lightly poached.

Corn Soup (*Con supu*)

Makes 4 servings
1 egg, ½ cup milk, 1 ham slice,
4 cups chicken stock, 1 can (400 g/13 oz) creamed corn, 1 tsp salt, dash of pepper, 1½ tbsp *katakuriko* or cornstarch

1 In a pot, combine chicken stock and creamed corn and bring to a boil. Season with salt and pepper. Add *katakuriko* dissolved in water. Cook a little longer.
2 Stir in beaten egg and milk. When the soup is nice and hot, ladle into small soup bowls. Mince ham and set atop soup as garnish.

Bean Thread Soup (*Harusame supu*)

Makes 4 servings
60 g/2 oz bean thread (*harusame*), 4 fresh *shiitake* mushrooms, ½ green onion, 2–3 slices fresh ginger, 2 tsp sesame oil, 50 g/2 oz ground chicken,
4 cups chicken stock, 1¼ tsp salt, 1 tsp soy sauce

1 Soak *harusame* in warm water to soften. Drain and cut into shorter lengths.
2 Thinly slice *shiitake* and green onion.
3 Stir-fry green onion and ginger in sesame oil. Add ground chicken and stir-fry. Add chicken stock, salt and soy sauce and bring to a boil. Add the *harusame* and cook for 2–3 minutes.

Sushi

Today, sushi, which dates back to the 10th century, is known throughout the world. Sushi comes in a variety of shapes and styles. For example, *chirashi zushi* is a scattered sushi dish in which the ingredients are carefully arranged on a bed of sushi rice. There is also *nigiri zushi* in which the sushi ingredients are placed on bite-sized molded rounds of rice; *maki zushi* in which sushi ingredients including the sushi rice are rolled together on a sheet of *yaki-nori*; *temaki zushi*, hand-rolled sushi; and *inari zushi* in which sushi rice and other ingredients are stuffed into *aburage* tofu puffs. There's room for creativity, as seen in Western style sushi dishes using fruit and such ingredients as ham to make sushi canapés.

Colorful Sushi (*Chirashi zushi*)

As you gently scoop beneath the fine scrambled shrimp (*ebi soboro*) and crêpe-like egg strips (*usuyaki tamago*), the colorful sushi rice emerges. There is a wonderful harmony between the light flavors of the ingredients scattered on top of this dish and the rich flavors of the ingredients mixed in with the sushi rice.

A few tips on how to make Colorful Sushi: first you must reconstitute the dried ingredients and prepare all the ingredients separately. Then cook the rice for making sushi rice. It is important to plan ahead when preparing this dish.

How to Make Sushi Rice

Makes 6 servings

3 rice cooker cups of uncooked rice
  * You will be using a little less water than usual to cook the rice (i.e.- 3³⁄₁₀ of a rice cooker cup of water)
10 cm/4 inch piece dried kelp (*kobu* or *konbu*)
Seasoned Vinegar:
  5 tablespoons rice vinegar
  3½ tablespoons sugar
  2 teaspoons salt

1 Wash the rice and let it drain in a colander at least one hour before cooking. Thirty minutes before cooking, place the rice in the rice cooker and add 3³⁄₁₀ rice cooker cups of water and the piece of cleaned sea kelp. Right before cooking, remove the sea kelp, and then switch on the rice cooker. When the rice has finished cooking, let it stay in the rice cooker for another 12–13 minutes. (Picture 1)

2 Combine the ingredients for the Seasoned Vinegar. Make sure that the sugar is completely dissolved. To clean the traditional wooden sushi bowl used in this recipe, wipe it with a damp cloth. (Picture 2)

3 Place the rice in the bowl and drizzle the Seasoned Vinegar over it. With a wooden paddle, cut into the rice (rather than mixing) to separate it and allow the Seasoned Vinegar to flavor the rice. While doing this, fan the rice to gradually cool it down. Place a well-wrung wet cloth over the mixture until you are ready to use it. (Pictures 3–4)

How to Prepare the Other Ingredients

Dried ingredients and carrot cooked in sweet broth:
6 dried *shiitake* mushrooms, soaked in water
   until soft (reserve water to use in broth)
15 g/½ oz dried gourd (*kampyo*)
Dash of salt
½ carrot (70 g/2½ oz)
Broth A:
   1 cup water, reserved from soaking *shiitake*
   1 tablespoon sugar
   1 tablespoon saké
   1 tablespoon *mirin*
   3 tablespoons soy sauce

Vinegared lotus root:
1 section lotus root (about 150 g/5 oz)
Sweet Vinegar A:
   3 tablespoons *dashi* stock
   3 tablespoons rice vinegar
   1 tablespoon sugar
   ⅕ teaspoon salt

Fine scrambled shrimp:
200 g/7 oz shrimp
1 teaspoon sugar
⅕ teaspoon salt
Drop of red food coloring

Sweet vinegared shrimp:
12 shrimp
Sweet Vinegar B:
   1 tablespoon *dashi* stock
   1 tablespoon rice vinegar
   1 teaspoon sugar
   ⅛ teaspoon salt

Crêpe-like egg strips:
2 eggs
Seasonings A:
   1 tablespoon saké
   1 teaspoon sugar
   ⅕ teaspoon salt
½ tablespoon salad oil

Snow peas:
50 g/1½ oz snow peas
½ teaspoon salt

Dried ingredients and carrot cooked in sweet broth:
1 Soak the *shiitake* mushrooms in water to reconstitute them. Remove and discard the stems. Quickly wash the dried gourd strips (*kanpyo*) and sprinkle with a dash of salt. Rub the salt in briskly to soften, then soak the gourd strips in water to reconstitute. Boil the gourd strips until they become transparent. Cut into pieces 3 cm/1¼ inch long and 5 cm/2 inch wide. Peel the carrot and cut into 3 cm/1¼ inch-long matchsticks.
2 Mix Broth A in a pot and then add the *shiitake* mushrooms. Cook for 5–6 minutes, and then remove the *shiitake* from the broth and set aside. Cook the gourd strips and carrot in the remaining broth for 5–6 minutes (until the broth has evaporated). Thinly slice the *shiitake*.

Vinegared lotus root:
1 Cut the lotus root into 4–5 cm/2 inch-long pieces so that it's easier to handle. To peel the lotus root pieces, make incisions lengthwise between the holes. As you peel each section (i.e. from one lengthwise incision to the next), you will also be carving a rounded arc, so that each slice will be shaped like a flower. Cut into 2–3 mm slices. Soak in vinegared water for 10 minutes.
2 Boil the lotus root slices for 1 minute. Quickly drain in a colander and then place in Sweet Vinegar A.

Fine scrambled shrimp:
1 Shell and devein the shrimp and quickly boil until pink. Cut shrimp into small pieces. Then mash in a mortar (*suribachi*). Place the shrimp in a small pot.
2 Add sugar, salt and a small dash of red food coloring powder dissolved in water. Heat the pot over low heat and mix with chopsticks, cooking until the mixture becomes dry and powdery.

Sweet vinegared shrimp:
1 Remove the heads from the shrimp and devein.
2 Quickly boil, then drain and let cool. Remove the shell and place in Sweet Vinegar B and set aside.

Crêpe-like egg strips:
1 Beat the eggs and add the saké, sugar and salt.
2 Heat a rectangular omelet pan. Add salad oil and pour in just enough egg to coat the pan. When the egg starts to bubble, break the bubbles with a chopstick. When the surface is dry, flip and continue cooking for 20–30 seconds. Prepare the remaining egg mixture in the same way. When the omelets have cooled, cut into 3 cm/1¼ inch-long strips.

Snow peas:
Remove the strings from the snow peas and quickly boil in 2–3 cups salted water until they turn a bright green. Immerse in cold water and drain in a colander. Slice diagonally into fine strips.

Mixing the Ingredients and Serving

While the sushi rice is still warm, mix in the *shiitake*, gourd and carrot mixture. (The ingredients will not mix well with cold rice.) First sprinkle the mixture over the rice and then mix it with the rice with a wooden paddle. Cover with a damp cloth until serving.

(Pictures 5–6, page 49)

Place the sushi rice in a serving dish and decorate with the remaining ingredients in the following order: fine scrambled shrimp, snow peas, vinegared lotus root, sweet vinegared shrimp and egg strips. Use a large serving dish for maximum visual impact.

Hand-Formed Sushi (*Nigiri zushi*)

Bite-sized pieces of hand-formed sushi rice topped with fresh *sashimi*.

Makes 4 servings

900 g/2 lb sushi rice, made from 2 rice cooker
  cups of rice, see page 49
100 g/3 oz *sashimi*-quality tuna
100 g/3½ oz *sashimi*-quality fluke
100 g/3½ oz boiled octopus
100 g/3½ oz smoked salmon
4 tablespoons salted salmon roe
8 sheets toasted *nori* (*yaki-nori*) 4 cm x 15 cm;
  1⅔ inch x 6 inch
1 teaspoon grated *wasabi* (Japanese horseradish) or *wasabi* paste
4 *shiso* leaves
Sliced sweet pickled ginger (*gari*)
3–4 tablespoons soy sauce

1 Cut the tuna, fluke, octopus and salmon into 5 mm/¼ inch slices. There should be 8 slices of each type of fish. (Picture 1)

2 Cool the sushi rice. Moisten your hands with vinegar and take about 25 g/1 oz of rice. Gently hold the rice and mold it into a rounded shape with your fingers. (Pictures 2–3)

3 Using one finger, place a small amount of *wasabi* on the rice ball. Place a slice of tuna atop the rice and press it down with two fingers while holding the rice ball in your other hand. Repeat this step for the rest of the tuna, fluke, octopus and salmon slices. (Pictures 4–5)

4 Make 8 rice balls according to the above instructions. Wrap a piece of toasted *nori* around the outside of each of these 8 rice balls. Place some salmon roe on top of each rice ball.

5 Place *shiso* leaves and sweet pickled ginger on four serving plates. Arrange 8 pieces of sushi on each plate. Serve the soy sauce in a small dish alongside. Dip each piece of sushi in soy sauce before eating.

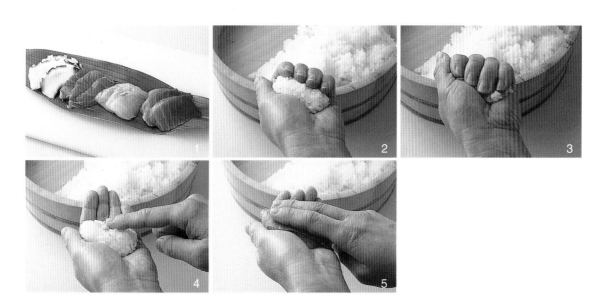

Beef *Tataki* Sushi (*Gyu tataki no nigiri zushi*)

Nigiri-style sushi topped with rare beef is becoming very popular in Japan.

Makes 6 servings

1.3 kg/3 lb sushi rice, made from 3 rice cooker
    cups of rice, see page 49
500 g/12 oz beef shank (whole)
Sauce:
    2 tablespoons soy sauce
    2 tablespoons *mirin*
    ⅔ tablespoon salad oil
3–4 tablespoons grated *wasabi* (Japanese
    horseradish)
20 g/⅔ oz young green onions (*me-negi*)
    or chives
7-8 slices sweet pickled ginger (*gari*)
6 small chrysanthemums for decoration

1 Cut the beef shank in half and firmly pierce all over with a fork. (Picture 1)

2 Heat a frying pan and add the salad oil. Brown the outside of the two pieces of beef over high heat. Add the sauce mixture to the pan and turn the beef frequently so that it is well covered with the sauce. Remove the beef from the pan and let it cool on a plate. Reserve the sauce.
(Pictures 2–3)

3 Slice the beef into 3 mm/⅛ inch slices.
(Picture 4)

4 Form the sushi rice into oval balls (appropriate for *nigiri-zushi*). Apply just enough pressure to allow the rice to hold together; the rice will be less tasty if you press too firmly. Use up all of the rice.

5 Place a rice ball in the palm of your hand. With the index finger of your other hand, take a little grated *wasabi* and spread it over the top of the rice ball. Then place a slice of beef over the rice and press down lightly with your index and middle fingers. Do the same for all the rice balls.
(Picture 5)

6 Place the sushi on a serving plate. Lightly brush the tops with the remaining sauce. Garnish with a small bunch of young green onions (all of equal length), sweet pickled ginger and a few chrysanthemums. (Picture 6)

Hand-Rolled Sushi (*Temaki zushi*)

A great dish for a party. You can set out the ingredients, sushi rice and *nori* at the dining table, and let your guests roll their own sushi.

Makes 6 servings

1.3 kg/3 lb sushi rice made from 3 rice cooker
  cups of rice, see page 49
100–150 g/3–5 oz *sashimi*-quality tuna
100 g/3 oz *sashimi*-quality cuttlefish
12 sweet shrimp
60 g/2 oz salmon roe
1 piece sweet salted cod roe (about 60 g/2 oz)
2 cucumbers
100 g/3⅓ oz *daikon* sprouts
10–20 *shiso* leaves
10–16 sheets toasted *nori* seaweed (*yaki-nori*)
  20 x 20 cm/4 x 4 inch
½ piece fresh *wasabi* (Japanese horseradish) or
  1 teaspoon grated *wasabi*
4–5 tablespoons soy sauce

1 Cut the tuna into 1 cm x 5–6 cm/½ inch x 2–2¼ inch pieces. Cut the cuttlefish into 5 mm x 5–6 cm/¼ inch x 2¼ inch strips.

2 Remove the shells from the shrimp, leaving the tails intact. Slice the cod roe diagonally into 5–6 mm/½ inch-thick pieces.

3 Cut the cucumber into 5–7 cm/ 2–3 inch lengths, then cut lengthwise into 5 mm/¼ inch sticks. Cut the radish sprouts off at their base. Cut the sheets of *nori* in half.

4 Arrange the ingredients mentioned above in Steps 1 to 3 on a large plate. Garnish with *shiso* leaves. Place the sushi rice in a bowl. Place the *nori*, soy sauce, and *wasabi* in separate dishes.

(picture 1)

5 Place a sheet of *nori* in the palm of your hand. Put some *sushi* rice on the *nori* and add a touch of *wasabi*. Add one item of seafood and a piece of vegetable. Roll the *nori* to form a cone shape. Dip in soy sauce before eating.   (Pictures 2–6)

Rolled Sushi (*Maki zushi*)

Once the ingredients are in place, roll the sushi quickly and with confidence.

Makes 6 servings

1.3 kg/3 lb sushi rice, made from 3 rice cooker cups of rice, see page 49
4 sheets toasted *nori* seaweed (*yaki-nori*)
20 g/⅔ oz dried gourd strips (*kampyo*)
Broth A:
  1½ cups *dashi* stock
  2½ tablespoons sugar
  2 tablespoons soy sauce
6 dried *shiitake* mushrooms
Broth B:
  1½ cups *dashi* stock
  1½ tablespoons sugar
  1½ tablespoons soy sauce

2 blocks of dried tofu (*koya-dofu*)
Broth C:
  2 cups *dashi* stock
  1½ tablespoons sugar
  1½ tablespoons light soy sauce
  ½ teaspoon salt
3 eggs
Seasoning A:
  3 tablespoons *dashi* stock
  1⅓ tablespoons sugar
  ⅕ teaspoon salt
  ¼ teaspoon soy sauce
Salad oil
1 bunch *mitsuba* trefoil
Sliced pickled red ginger

1 Place Broth A in a pot. Bring to a boil and add the dried gourd strips. Cook well and remove from the broth. When the gourd strips have cooled, cut them the same lengths as the *nori* sheets.

2 Soak the dried *shiitake* in water to reconstitute. Remove and discard the stems. Cook well in Broth B. Remove from the broth. When the *shiitake* have cooled down, cut them into 5 mm/¼ inch-wide slices.

3 Soak the dried tofu (*koya-dofu*) in warm water to fully reconstitute it. Then squeeze to remove the excess water. Cover with a drop lid and cook slowly in Broth C. Remove from the broth and let cool. Cut into 1 cm/½ inch-square bars.

4 To prepare the omelet, beat the eggs and add Seasoning A. Cook in a rectangular omelet pan coated with salad oil to make a thick omelet. Cut into 1 cm/½ inch square bars.

5 Boil the *mitsuba* trefoil just until it turns deep green. Remove and gently squeeze to remove excess water.

6 Divide the sushi rice into four equal parts. (You can usually make 4 rolls with 3 cups of rice, i.e. about 250–270 g/8–9 oz per roll).

7 Roll the sushi according to the photographs. For each sushi roll, place a sheet of *nori* on top of a bamboo sushi rolling mat. Spread the rice out evenly over the *nori* (leave about 2 cm/⅔ inch of space at the upper edge). Place a quarter of the ingredients neatly in the middle of the rice. Then pick up the edge of the bamboo mat and start rolling away from you, until the edges of the *nori* meet. Press down firmly to seal and then remove the bamboo mat. Cut into 1.5 cm/⅔ inch pieces, place on a serving dish and garnish with pickled red ginger.

(Pictures 1–9)

Tofu Puffs Stuffed with Sushi Rice (*Inari zushi*)

The sweet and salty flavors of the deep-fried tofu pouches combined with the sweetness of the sushi rice create a beautiful harmony.

Makes 6 servings
1.3 kg/3 lb sushi rice, made from 3 rice cooker
  cups of rice, see page 49
Sushi rice mixture:
  100 g/3¼ oz of carrot
  150 g/5 oz boiled bamboo shoots
Cooking Broth:
  1 cup *dashi* stock
  1 tablespoon *mirin*
½ teaspoon salt
2 tablespoons toasted white sesame seeds

Deep-fried tofu pouches:
9 pieces tofu puffs (*aburage*)
2 cups *dashi* stock
Seasoning Mix A:
  4½ tablespoons sugar
  3 tablespoons saké
  4 tablespoons soy sauce
  1 tablespoon *mirin*
Pickled red ginger, sliced

1 Place the individual *aburage* pieces on a cutting board. Using a wooden pestle (*surikogi*), roll over the pieces firmly. (This will make it easier to open the *aburage*). Cut the pieces in half and gently pull apart each piece, thus forming a pouch. Place in boiling water for 2–3 minutes, to remove excess oil.   (Pictures 1–2)
2 To flavor the deep-fried tofu pouches, place the *dashi* stock and *aburage* in a pot and cook for 15 minutes. Add Seasoning Mix A, cover with a drop lid and continue to cook until the sauce is greatly reduced.
3 To make the sushi rice mixture: Peel the carrot. Cut the carrot and bamboo shoots into 1.5 cm/⅔ inch-length pieces. Cook in the Cooking Broth for 5 minutes. Drain.
4 Toast the sesame seeds again in a frying pan to bring out their flavor.
5 Mix the carrots, bamboo shoots and sesame seeds with the sushi rice. Divide the sushi rice into 16 portions (or one portion for each *aburage* pouch).
6 Lightly squeeze any remaining excess water from the *aburage*, and stuff each one carefully with the sushi rice mixture. Place on a serving dish and garnish with sliced pickled red ginger.

(Pictures 3–6)

Salmon Sushi (*Sake zushi*)

Use good quality salmon, since you're only using a small amount.

Makes 6 servings
1.3 kg/3 lb sushi rice, made from 3 rice cooker cups of rice, see page 49
3 pieces (about 140 g/4⅔ oz) of sweetened salted salmon (*amajio-zake*)
3 cucumbers
⅓ teaspoon salt
20 green *shiso* leaves
2 tablespoons toasted white sesame seeds

1 Grill the salmon, without burning it. Remove the skin, bones and dark colored flesh and break into large flakes.
2 Thinly slice the cucumbers and sprinkle with salt. Let stand. Squeeze to remove excess water.
3 Place the *shiso* leaves together and thinly slice them into fine strips. Place in cold water, then dry with a paper towel.
4 Toast sesame seeds again to bring out their flavor.
5 Mix salmon and cucumber with sushi rice. Place in individual serving dishes, sprinkle sesame seeds over each serving and garnish with thinly sliced *shiso* leaves.

* For variety, try horse mackerel (*aji*) or barracuda (*kamasu*) instead of salmon.

Chinese-Style Slices of Raw Fish Over Sushi Rice
(*Chukafu sashimi zushi*)

Makes 4 servings

900 g/2 lb sushi rice, made from 2 rice cooker
cups of rice, see page 49

300 g/10 oz *sashimi*-quality white fish,
e.g. sea bream (*tai*) or halibut (*hirame*)

Sauce:
½ tablespoon toasted sesame seeds, ground
¼ teaspoon salt
Dash of pepper
1½ tablespoons soy sauce
1 tablespoon sesame oil

1 cucumber
⅓ carrot (about 40 g/1⅓ oz)
½ stalk celery
½ green onion
Few sprigs of fresh coriander

Mixture for Lemon-Soy Sauce:
1 tablespoon lemon juice
1 tablespoon soy sauce

1 Thinly slice the cucumber at a diagonal, to
form 3–4 cm/1⅔ inch long slices. Then julienne.
(This way, each stick retains a bit of the beautiful dark green edge of the peel). Cut the green
onion, carrot and celery in the same way to create 3–4 cm/1⅔ inch long match sticks. Place the
vegetables (separately) in cold water.

2 Thinly slice the fish. Mix the sauce ingredients. Toss the fish slices with the sauce.

3 Evenly divide the sushi rice into four individual serving bowls. Place the vegetables in a circle
atop the rice. Place the fish in the center of each
bowl and garnish with sprigs of coriander.
Before eating, each guest should pour some of
the lemon-soy sauce mixture over his or her
serving, and mix well.

Sweet Shrimp and Avocado Over Sushi Rice
(*Ama ebi to abokado no sushi*)

For those who like this unique combination, this sushi is unforgettably delicious.

Makes 4 servings
900 g/2 lb sushi rice, made from 2 rice
  cooker cups of rice, see page 49
400 g/13 oz sweet shrimp (*ama ebi*)
2 avocados
1 tablespoon lemon juice
¼ cucumber
20 g/⅔ oz *murame* (red *shiso* buds), if desired
¼ lemon
2 tablespoons grated *wasabi* (Japanese
  horseradish)
2 tablespoons soy sauce

1 Remove the heads and shells (except for the tail) from the sweet shrimp.
2 Cut the avocados lengthwise in half. Remove the pits and peel. Mash with a fork and toss with the lemon juice.
3 Place the *sushi* rice into individual serving bowls. Place the sweet shrimp and mashed avocado over the rice. Garnish with sliced cucumber, *murame* and lemon wedges. Squeeze the lemon over the dish before eating. When you eat, dip each bite into a small side dish of soy sauce and *wasabi*.

Raw Tuna Over Sushi Rice (*Maguro no tekone zushi fu*)

A dynamic sushi dish featuring raw tuna in a ginger soy sauce.

Makes 4 servings
900 g/2 lb sushi rice, made from 2 rice cooker cups of rice, see page 49
300 g/10 oz *sashimi* quality tuna
Sauce:
   2 tablespoons soy sauce
   1 tablespoon *mirin* (sweet rice wine)
   1 tablespoon grated ginger
½ sheet toasted *nori* seaweed (*yaki nori*)
4–5 *shiso* stems with buds (*ho-jiso*)

1 Cut the tuna into 7–8 mm/⅓ inch-thick bite-sized pieces. Coat with the sauce, and let stand for 5–6 minutes.
2 With scissors, cut the *nori* into thin strips, 2–3 cm/1–1¼ inch long. Remove the buds from the *shiso* stems.

3 Place the sushi rice in individual serving bowls. Sprinkle the *nori* evenly over the rice. Remove the tuna from the sauce and place over the rice. Sprinkle with *shiso* buds.

* *Tekone-zushi*, or hand mixed sushi, originated in Wakayama prefecture. Traditionally, cooks use their hands to mix *sashimi*-quality bonito seasoned with ginger soy sauce with sushi rice. For this recipe, you may use your hands to mix the tuna with the rice. If you do, sprinkle the *nori* over the sushi after it has been mixed. For variation, try grated *wasabi* (Japanese horseradish) soy sauce, instead of ginger soy sauce. You may substitute the leaves of the green *shiso* (*ao-jiso*) if the buds are not available.

Western-Style Sushi *(Yofu zushi)*

This sushi uses lemon juice and salad oil.

Makes 6 servings
3 cups of uncooked Japanese style rice
Seasoned Vinegar Mixture:
   5 tablespoons lemon juice
   2 tablespoons salad oil
   1 tablespoon salt
   Dash of pepper
150 g/5 oz shrimp
   1 teaspoon saké
   ⅕ teaspoon salt
100 g/3¼ oz smoked salmon
1 bunch fresh green asparagus
1 small papaya
1 head green leaf lettuce

1 Cook the rice with about 10% more water than usual, so that it is not as sticky. Steam the boiled rice for 12–13 minutes. Mix the cooked rice with the Seasoned Vinegar Mixture to make sushi rice (see page 49). The oil will coat each grain, making it less sticky.

2 Shell the shrimp, removing the tails, and devein. Toss with saké and a dash of salt and let sit for 10 minutes. Plunge the shrimp into boiling water for a few seconds and remove with a slotted spoon.

3 Cut off the ends of the asparagus and place in boiling water until the stalks turn bright green. Place in cold water and then cut into 3 cm/1 inch-long pieces.

4 Cut the smoked salmon into bite-sized pieces.

5 Cut the papaya lengthwise in thirds and remove the flesh with a spoon. Cut into 2 cm/1 inch cubes.

6 Mix the sushi rice together with the shrimp, asparagus, smoked salmon and papaya and then place in a serving dish on a decorative bed of green leaf lettuce.

Curry-Flavored Sushi (*Kare zushi*)

This sushi is sure to whet your appetite even on a hot summer day.

Makes 6 servings
3 cups rice
Vinegar Mixture:
   3½ tablespoons rice vinegar
   3½ tablespoons salad oil
   1 tablespoon curry powder
   ¾ teaspoon salt
   Dash of pepper
100 g/3⅓ oz thinly sliced ham
100 g/3⅓ oz boiled octopus
6 radishes
60 g/2 oz canned corn

1 Cook the rice with less water than usual (about 110%). Once cooked, let the rice stand for 12–13 minutes. Pour the Vinegar Mixture over the rice and mix very well to blend the flavors.

2 Cut the ham into 1.5 cm/½ inch squares. Thinly slice the boiled octopus and then cut into 1.5 cm/½ inch squares.

3 Cut the radishes in half and then cut into small triangular wedges. Drain the canned corn very well.

4 Sprinkle the ingredients mentioned in Steps 2 and 3 over the sushi rice and then mix well.

Small Clear Soups

Hot clear soup goes well with sushi since,
unlike other rice dishes, sushi is served
at room temperature.

Clear Soup with Fish Cake and *Shimeji* Mushrooms
(*Kamaboko to shimeji no suimono*)

Makes 4 servings
1 (4 cm/1⅔ inch) piece fish cake (*kamaboko*), ½
bunch *shimeji* mushrooms, 4 snow peas,
4 cups *dashi* stock, ¼ tsp salt, 2 tsp soy sauce

1 Cut a piece of *kamaboko* in half lengthwise
(from top and bottom) and then into 5 mm/¼
inch slices.
2 Roughly break apart half the *shimeji*.
3 Quickly boil snow peas, and then slice.
4 Bring *dashi* stock to a boil. Season with salt and
soy sauce. Add the *shimeji* mushrooms, and continue to cook for 1–2 minutes. Add the fish cake
slices and cook for 20–30 seconds.
5 Ladle the soup into four small individual soup
bowls and garnish with snow peas.

Clear Soup with Pickled Plum and Seaweed (*Ume tororo sui*)

Makes 4 servings
Pinch of *shirasuboshi* (dried young sardines),
pinch of *tororokobu* (fine sheets of seaweed), 1
pickled plum,
4 cups *dashi* stock, small amount of *daikon* sprouts

1 Place *shirasuboshi* and *tororokobu* in four small
individual soup bowls. Tear apart pickled plum
into four pieces and place in the soup bowls.
2 Bring *dashi* stock to a boil and ladle into each
soup bowl. Cut the tops from *daikon* sprouts and
use as a garnish for each serving.

Clear Soup with Puffy Fish Cake Balls and Ginger
(*Hanpen to shoga no suimono*)

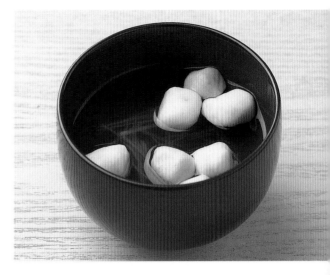

Makes 4 servings

30 red fish cake balls (*arare hanpen*)or 1 piece of *hanpen*, 4–5 slices ginger, 4 cups *dashi* stock,1¼ tsp salt, 2 tsp soy sauce

1 If fish cake balls not available, cut *hanpen* into 1 cm/½ inch cubes.

2 Shred ginger. Bring *dashi* stock to a boil. Season with salt and soy sauce. Add fish cake balls and ginger and continue cooking for 20–30 seconds.

Egg Flower Soup (*Kakitama jiru*)

Makes 4 servings

8 sprigs *mitsuba* trefoil, 4 cups *dashi* stock, 1¼ tsp salt, 2 tsp soy sauce, 1 tbsp *katakuriko*, 2 eggs

1 For each serving, tie *mitsuba* trefoil together in the middle to make four pieces.

2 Bring *dashi* stock to a boil. Season with salt and soy sauce. Dissolve *katakuriko* in water, and add to the soup to thicken it.

3 Beat eggs and gently pour them into the soup, while stirring, to form egg flowers.

4. Ladle into four small soup bowls. Garnish with the trefoil ties.

Crab Soup (*Kani no oboro jiru*)

Makes 4 servings

1 small can (100g/3¼ oz) crab meat, 4 cups *dashi* stock, ⅔ salt, 1 tsp soy sauce, 2 tbsp *katakuriko*, ½ green onion

1 Remove and discard the soft bones and cartilage from the crab meat and chop up the remaining meat.

2 Add the crab meat to the *dashi* stock and bring to a boil. Skim off the scum. Season with salt and soy sauce. Dissolve *katakuriko* in water, and add to the soup to thicken it.

3 Ladle into four small individual soup bowls. Garnish with a diagonal slice of green onion.

Japanese Lunch Boxes and Bowls

Bento or *obento* lunch boxes refer to portable dishes. People often bring lunch boxes on a trip, or when they go hiking or driving. *Donburi-mono* is a simple type of dish in which various side dishes featuring ingredients such as seafood, meat, vegetables and eggs are served atop rice in deep bowls.

Shokado Lunch Box (*Shokado bento*)

Shokado is a rectangular or square Japanese-style lunch box made of lacquered wood. There are sections within the lunch box to hold different foods. Usually rice is placed in one section while the other sections contain favorite side dishes including *sashimi*, grilled fish or *nimono* (simmered) dishes. A *shokado* lunch box is appropriate even for casual occasions.

Makes 4 servings
Sashimi:
200 g/7 oz *sashimi* quality tuna
80 g/3 oz cuttlefish
60 g/2 oz *daikon* radish
½ cucumber
4 *shiso* leaves
4 *shiso* stems, which contain buds
1 teaspoon grated *wasabi* (Japanese
   horseradish)

1 Select a rectangular piece of tuna for this dish. Place the tuna lengthwise on a cutting board and cut it horizontally into 1 cm/½ inch slices.
2 Cut the cuttlefish into strips 5 cm/2 inch long and 7–8 mm/⅜ inch wide.
3 Cut the *daikon* radish and cucumber into match sticks. Soak in cold water and then let dry.
4 Mound the cucumber and *daikon* radish matchsticks in the center of one section of the

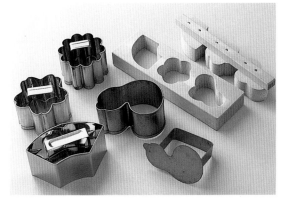

*Mosso-gata**

lunch box and place *shiso* leaves around the vegetables. Place the tuna slices and cuttlefish strips facing forward. Garnish with the *shiso* buds and *wasabi* horseradish. Top with soy sauce before eating.

Nimono Dish:
200 g/7 oz chicken breast
150 g/5 oz boiled bamboo shoots
1 carrot
6 small dried *shiitake* mushrooms
3 tablespoons salad oil
3 cups *dashi* stock
2 tablespoons saké
Seasonings Mix A:
   4 tablespoons soy sauce
   3 tablespoons sugar
   3 tablespoons *mirin*
10–12 snow peas
   ½ teaspoon salt

1 Dice the chicken into 3 cm/1¼ inch cubes. Chop the bamboo shoots and carrot into similarly sized pieces. To reconstitute the dried *shiitake* mushrooms, soak them in water. Remove and discard the stems and slice.
2 Heat the salad oil in a pot. Stir-fry the chicken until it is no longer pink. Add the carrot, *shiitake* mushrooms, and bamboo shoots (in that order) and stir-fry. Add *dashi* stock and saké and continue cooking for another 5 minutes.
3 Add Seasoning Mix A to the pot. Cover the surface of the mixture with aluminum foil or cooking paper. Cook for 10–15 minutes.
4 Remove the strings from the snow peas and quickly boil in 2–3 cups of salted water. Drain the peas and cut them in half at a diagonal. Scatter the snow peas over the mixture.

Teriyaki Fish:
4 pieces fresh salmon (320 g–400 g/11–13 oz)
Marinade B:
   3 tablespoons soy sauce
   1½ tablespoons saké

1½ tablespoons sugar
1 tablespoon salad oil
4 sweetened chestnuts

1 Mix Marinade B. Cut each piece of salmon in half and marinate for 10–15 minutes, turning the pieces over once after about 5 minutes.
2 Heat the salad oil in a frying pan. Place the salmon face down and brown the surface over high heat. Turn the pieces over and continue to cook the same way.
3 Reduce the heat to medium. Add the remaining Marinade B. Continue cooking while shaking the frying pan to coat the fish with the sauce. Use a spoon to coat the salmon with the sauce, once it has been reduced. Continue coating the fish until the pieces glisten.
4 Arrange the teriyaki salmon in one section of the lunch box. Place sweetened chestnuts in front of the fish.

Shaped Rice:
300 g/⅔ lb cooked rice
1 teaspoon toasted black sesame seeds

1 Dip a *mosso*-type rice mold in hot water to moisten the inside. Divide the rice into 4 equal portions and place a portion into the mold.
(Pictures 1–2)
2 Press the rice down with the palm of your hand to flatten the surface. Insert the other half of the mold and press down firmly. Then remove the rice from the mold.   (Pictures 3–5)
3 For a pleasing taste and appearance, sprinkle some sesame seeds over the rice.

* *Mosso-gata* is a rice mold. The molds come in a variety of shapes: flower shapes featuring chrysanthemums, cherry blossoms and plum blossoms; gourd shapes and molds shaped like fans. They are usually made of wood or stainless steel. There are two parts to the mold: a frame which holds rice and another piece which pushes the rice out of the mold into a certain shape.

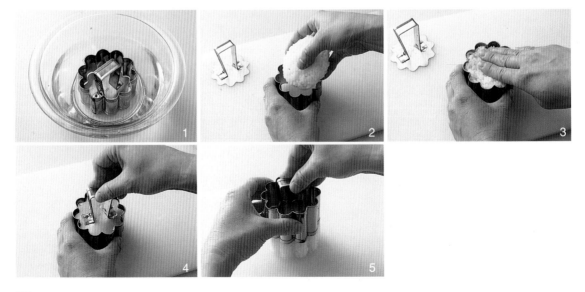

Rice Ball Lunch Box (*Onigiri bento*)

Rice balls shaped with salted hands are referred to as *onigiri*. *Onigiri* are wonderful to take along on a picnic, because they are easy to eat and they keep well.

Rice Balls (*Onigiri*)

Makes 4 servings
12 Rice Balls
1 kg/2 lb cooked rice
2 large *umeboshi* (Japanese pickled plums)
1 small piece salted salmon, 70–80 g/2-3 oz
1 small piece cod roe, 70 g/2 oz

2 pieces toasted seaweed (*yaki-nori*)
  20 x 20 cm/4 x 4 inch
½ teaspoon salt

1 Remove and discard the pits of the *umeboshi*, and roughly tear the *umeboshi* in half. Grill the salted salmon. Remove and discard the skin and bones, then break the salmon meat into flakes. Fry the cod roe until cooked through. Cut it into 2–3 cm/1 inch-long pieces.
2 Divide a sheet of toasted *nori* seaweed into either six 20 cm/8 inch long strips or six rectangles, so that there are a total of 12 pieces.

73

3 Place about 80 g/3 oz of cooked rice in a bowl. To prevent the rice from sticking, moisten your hands with water. Place a pinch of salt in your palm and rub the salt gently into your hands. Then pick up the rice.   (Pictures 1–3)

4 Gently form the rice into a ball with cupped hands. With a finger, make an indentation in the middle and place a piece of *umeboshi* inside. Press the rice firmly together, covering over the hole. Bend the fingers of one hand so that they are aligned. Use your fingers to form the rice into a triangular shape, rotating the rice ball as you press firmly.   (Picture 4)

5 Following the above procedure, make four *onigiri* for each of the ingredients, i.e., *umeboshi*, salmon and cod roe. Wrap a piece of *yaki nori* around each *onigiri*. If you are using long strips, wrap each piece lengthwise around the edge of the onigiri. If you are using rectangular pieces of *yaki-nori*, place each piece across one edge of the *onigiri*, so that it covers both faces.

Flavorful Japanese Fried Chicken

2 large chicken thighs, 500 g/1 lb
1 tablespoon saké
2 tablespoons soy sauce
1 teaspoon ginger juice
3 tablespoons *katakuriko* or cornstarch
3 tablespoons flour
Oil for deep-frying

1 Cut the chicken into 4 cm/1½ inch cubes and marinate in a mixture of saké, soy sauce and ginger juice for 30 minutes.

2 When taking the chicken pieces out of the marinade, be sure to shake off excess liquid. Coat the chicken in a mixture of *katakuriko* and flour. Slowly deep-fry the chicken pieces in oil which has been heated to 170°C/350°F. For the last minute of cooking, turn the heat up so that the oil reaches 190°C/375°F.

Fresh Vegetables

Cut salad greens, tomatoes and cucumbers into whatever shape you like. Fresh vegetables are used to garnish fried chicken and omelets (see page 126) in lunch boxes.

Deep-Fried Seafood and Vegetables Over Rice (*Kakiage-don*)

Individual portions of chopped vegetables are deep-fried with seafood as the crowning glory of this dish.

Makes 4 servings
4-6 cups cooked rice (made from
　2 rice cooker cups of rice)
Kakiage:
20 prawns or jumbo shrimp
80 g/3 oz frozen cuttlefish
40 g/1⅓ oz carrot
20 g/⅔ oz trefoil (*mitsuba*)
Batter:
　1 egg and cold water to make 1 cup
　1 cup flour
　Dash of salt
2 tablespoons flour
Oil for deep-frying
Sauce:
　1 cup *dashi* stock
　2½ tablespoons sugar
　2½ tablespoons *mirin*
　Full ⅓ cup and a little more soy sauce

1 To make *kakiage*, remove the heads, tails and shells from the prawns and then devein. Cut the cuttlefish into 4–5 mm slices. Cut the carrots into matchsticks 3 cm/1¼ inch long and 3 mm/⅛ inch thick.

2 Begin heating the oil. Meanwhile, prepare the batter for deep-frying. Beat the egg well and add cold water to make 1 cup. Place the beaten egg mixture in a bowl and add the flour and a dash of salt. Mix lightly, being careful not to overmix.

3 Place a quarter of the ingredients from Step 1 into a smaller bowl. Toss with ½ tablespoon of flour. Then add some batter to thinly coat the whole mixture. When the oil reaches 180°C/360°F, gently slide the mixture into the hot oil. When the seafood and vegetables float to the top, gently poke with a chopstick to allow them to cook throughout. Flip the *kakiage* and remove when it is golden brown. Continue preparing the *kakiage* in the same way for the

three remaining servings.   (Pictures 1–5)

4 Bring the Sauce to a boil in a small pot.

5 Divide the rice among four deep individual serving bowls (*donburi*) and top each with one *kakiage*. Pour Sauce over each serving.

(Picture 6)

Asari Clams Over Rice (*Fukagawa-don*)

This dish of clams cooked in a *miso*-based sauce originated in the Fukagawa district of Tokyo.

Makes 4 servings
4–6 cups cooked rice
300 g/⅔ lb shelled littleneck clams (*asari*)
6 fresh *shiitake* mushrooms
2 green onions
1 piece fresh ginger, 10 g /⅓ oz
Cooking Liquid:
   1½ cups *dashi* stock
   3 tablespoons saké
   6 tablespoons *miso*
   1 tablespoon sugar
   1 tablespoon *mirin*
½ sheet of toasted seaweed (*yaki-nori*)

1 Place the shelled *asari* clams in a colander. Wash in salted water and drain well.
2 Cut the stems from the *shiitake* mushrooms and then slice each mushroom into 4–6 pieces. Cut the green onion into 2 cm/⅔ inch lengths. Thinly slice the ginger.
3 Pour the *dashi* stock and saké into a pot and then add the *shiitake*, green onions and ginger. When the mixture reaches a boil, dissolve the *miso* into the broth. Add the sugar and *mirin*.
4 Add the *asari* clams and cook until they begin to swell.
5 Divide the warm rice among four deep individual serving bowls (*donburi*) and then ladle equal portions of the clam mixture over the rice. Sprinkle toasted nori over each dish before serving.

Chicken and Egg Over Rice (*Oyako-don*)

Chicken and egg represent the "parent and child" (*oyako*) in this dish's name. The key to this recipe is in the combination of sweet and flavorful.

Makes 4 servings
4–6 cups cooked rice
350 g/12 oz chicken
100 g/3½ oz *shimeji* mushrooms
1½ green onions
50 g/2 oz *mitsuba* trefoil
Cooking Broth:
  1⅔ cups *dashi* stock
  2½ tablespoons sugar
  2½ tablespoons *mirin*
  5 tablespoons (or more) soy sauce
4 eggs

1 Cut the chicken into bite-sized pieces.
2 Cut the *shimeji* mushrooms off near their base and separate them. Cut the green onions into 3 cm/1¼ inch lengths, then slice in half. Cut the trefoil into 3 cm/1¼ inch lengths.
3 Beat the eggs in a bowl and set aside.
4 Place the Cooking Broth in a frying pan and bring to a boil. Add the chicken and *shimeji* mushrooms, and cook until the chicken is done. Toss in the green onions and cook for 1 minute.
5 Add the trefoil to the mixture and then add the eggs. Cover and cook for another 10–15 seconds, then remove from heat. Keep the frying pan covered and allow the eggs to continue cooking until they are half-cooked.
6 Divide the warm rice among four deep individual serving bowls (*donburi*) and place equal amounts of the chicken and egg mixture over the rice with a large spoon, making sure to include enough sauce for each serving.

Deep-Fried Pork Cutlet Over Rice (*Katsu-don*)

A hearty dish to satisfy both your taste buds and stomach.

Makes 4 servings
4–6 cups cooked rice
4 boneless pork cutlets (400 g/1 lb)
Dash of salt
Dash of pepper
Batter:
   30–40 g/1 oz flour
   1 egg
   50–60 g/2 oz bread crumbs
Oil for deep-frying
1 onion (about 150 g/5 oz)
⅓ cup frozen green peas
Cooking Broth:
   1½ cups *dashi* stock
   2½ tablespoons *mirin*
   2½ tablespoons sugar
   5 tablespoons soy sauce
4 eggs

1 To prepare the pork cutlets; make small slashes across the fatty edge at 1.5 cm/½ inch intervals. Salt and pepper the filets. Then coat with flour, dip in egg and coat with bread crumbs.
2 Heat the oil for deep-frying to 180°C/360°F. Deep-fry the pork until golden brown.
3 Cut the deep-fried cutlets into 1.5 cm/½ inch strips.
4 Cut the onion in half lengthwise and cut into 2–3 mm/½ inch slices. Place the green peas in a colander and pour boiling water over them.
5 Beat the eggs in a bowl lightly and set aside.
6 Place the cooking broth and onion slices in a frying pan and bring to a boil. Cook until the onions are soft.
7 Place the pork cutlets over the onion mixture and return to a boil. Pour the beaten eggs over the cutlets and add the green peas. Quickly cover and cook for another 10–15 seconds. Remove from heat and keep covered, until the egg is half-cooked.
8 Divide the rice among four deep individual serving bowls (*donburi*) and then ladle equal portions of the pork cutlet mixture over the rice.

Tricolored Rice (*Sanshoku soboro-don*)

Color, taste and texture make for a splendid variety in this all-time favorite.

Makes 4 servings
4–6 cups cooked rice
300 g/10 oz ground chicken
Seasoning Mix A:
  1 tablespoon sugar
  1 tablespoon *mirin*
  3 tablespoons soy sauce
  1 teaspoon ginger juice
8 eggs
Seasoning Mix B:
  ½ teaspoon salt
  2 tablespoons sugar
  1 teaspoon rice vinegar
70 g/2½ oz snow peas
Seasoning Mix C:
  ½ cup *dashi* stock
  1 teaspoon sugar
  ⅖ teaspoon salt
  ½ teaspoon soy sauce
30 g/1 oz sweet pickled ginger for garnish

1 To make the chicken: put the ground chicken into a pan and add Seasoning Mix A. Heat the pan and mix the ingredients with chopsticks. Cook until chicken becomes dry and flaky. Set aside.

2 To make the scrambled eggs: Beat the eggs in the pan and add Seasoning Mix B. Heat the pan and mix with chopsticks. Lower the heat as the egg mixture is cooked. Continue until the eggs are crumbly. (To avoid burning the eggs, remove the pan once in a while and place on a wet cloth.)

3 Snap off the ends of the snow peas and remove the strings. Parboil, then plunge the snow peas into cold water. Bring Seasoning Mix C to a boil. Add the snow peas and cook for a short time. Thinly slice the snow peas.

4 Divide the rice among four deep individual serving bowls (*donburi*) and place equal portions of the eggs, chicken and snow peas over the rice. Garnish with pickled sweet ginger.

Beef Over Rice (*Gyu-don*)

For a home-style touch add *shirataki* (*konnyaku* noodles). Remember to add the beef last.

Makes 4 servings
4–6 cups cooked rice
300 g/⅔ lb thinly sliced beef
1 onion (150 g/5 oz)
350 g/11 oz *shirataki*
½ bunch scallions or green onions
Cooking broth:
   1 cup *dashi* stock
   3 tablespoons sugar
   ⅓ cup saké
   ½ cup soy sauce
   2 tablespoons *mirin*

1 Cut the beef into bite-sized pieces.
2 Cut the onion in half lengthwise and then cut into 5 mm/¼ inch-thick slices. Boil *shirataki* fil-aments and cut them into shorter threads.
3 Cut the scallions into 3–4 cm/1½ inch lengths.
4 Cook the cooking broth, *shirataki* and onions in a pot until the onions are soft.
5 Add the beef and cook quickly to heat through. Add the scallions and cook for 20–30 seconds.
6 Divide the warm rice among four deep individual serving bowls (*donburi*) and top with equal amounts of the beef mixture. Thicken the remaining sauce over a high flame and then pour over the beef.

* You may add a beaten egg while the beef is still cooking or add an egg directly to each serving while still steaming hot.

Teriyaki Chicken with Egg Over Rice (*Kijiyaki-don*)

Sweetened scrambled eggs bring out the flavor in this dish.

Makes 4 servings
4-6 cups cooked rice
2 small chicken thighs (about 400 g/1 lb)
1½ tablespoons + ½ tablespoon salad oil
Sauce:
    1 tablespoon sugar
    5 tablespoons soy sauce
    3 tablespoons *mirin*
4 eggs
    ⅕ teaspoon salt
    ½ tablespoon sugar
2 tablespoons + ½ tablespoon salad oil
4 fresh *shiitake* mushrooms

12 *shishito* peppers or 4 sweet green peppers
¼ teaspoon salt
Dash of pepper
Dash of seven-spice pepper

1 Pierce the chicken skin all over with a fork, so that the meat can cook all the way through.
2 Beat the eggs and add the salt and sugar.
3 Remove the stems from the *shiitake* mushrooms and slice into halves. Gently score the *shishito* peppers lengthwise.
4 This meal can be prepared quickly, using only one frying pan. First, heat the frying pan and add 2 tablespoons of salad oil. Pour the beaten eggs into the pan. When the eggs start bubbling, scramble them and remove to a dish.
5 Quickly clean the frying pan and add a little salad oil. Add the *shiitake* mushrooms and peppers and stir-fry. Season with salt and pepper and put them aside.
6 Quickly rinse out the frying pan, add 1½ tablespoons of salad oil and place the chicken in the pan, with the skin side face down. Brown the chicken skin well. Then turn the chicken over and cook for another 2 minutes. Pour off the excess oil from the frying pan. In a small bowl, mix the sugar, soy sauce and *mirin* and add this mixture to the frying pan. Cover and cook over low heat for 6–7 minutes. Then, remove the lid and turn the heat up to reduce the sauce. Coat the chicken in the pan with this thickened sauce. Remove the chicken from the pan and slice into bite-sized pieces.
7 Divide the warm rice among four deep individual serving bowls (*donburi*) and then top with equal amounts of the scrambled eggs and chicken. Garnish with *shiitake* mushrooms and *shishito* peppers. Sprinkle with seven-spice pepper before serving.

Steak Over Rice (*Suteki-don*)

This *donburi* is flavored with butter and soy sauce.

Makes 4 servings
4–6 cups cooked rice
4 thick beef steaks (about 500 g/1 lb)
  ½ teaspoon salt
  Dash of pepper
2 cloves garlic
1–2 tablespoons salad oil
Seasoning Mix A:
  ¼ teaspoon salt
  ½ teaspoon soy sauce
  dash of pepper
1 stalk celery
1 bunch watercress
½ tablespoon salad oil
2 tablespoons butter
Seasoning Mix B:
  4 tablespoons soy sauce
  1½ tablespoons *mirin*
1 cup grated *daikon* radish
2–3 leaves *shiso*, a small amount
  finely cut into threads

1 Score the steaks along their fatty parts and season with salt and pepper. Thinly slice the garlic.

2 Remove and discard the fibrous veins in the stalk of celery and then thinly cut the celery at a diagonal. Remove the tough parts of the stems of the watercress and then chop.

3 Heat up a frying pan, add ½ tablespoon of salad oil and stir in the celery and watercress. Add Seasoning Mix A. Remove from the pan and put aside.

4 Quickly clean the frying pan and heat again. Add 1 tablespoon (or slightly more) salad oil and stir-fry the garlic until it turns a crispy brown. Place the beef in the pan and brown both sides over a high heat. Drain off the excess oil. Add the butter and Seasoning Mix B. Cover and cook 1–2 minutes over low heat.

5. Divide rice among four deep individual serving bowls (*donburi*). Thinly slice the beef into bite-sized pieces, and place it over the rice. Place the celery and watercress in the bowls. Pour the remaining sauce from the pan over each dish. Drain most of the water from the grated daikon radish and place in the center of each bowl. Garnish with *shiso* leaves.

Instant Pickles

The flavors of *donburi-mono* are usually quite rich,
so lightly flavored pickles provide a refreshing accompaniment.
These easy instant pickles take only 30 minutes
to prepare.

Pickled Eggplant in Spicy Soy Sauce
(*Nasu no karashijoyu zuke*)

Makes 4 servings
3 Asian eggplants, 1 tsp salt
Mustard Dressing Mix: 1 tsp Japanese mustard, 2
tsp rice vinegar, 2 tsp sugar, 1 tbsp soy sauce

1 Cut eggplants into quarters lengthwise and then
cut into 1 cm/½ inch cubes. Wash and rub the eggplant cubes with salt. Cover with a weight until the
eggplant becomes limp. Quickly rinse and squeeze
out the excess water.
2 Mix Mustard Dressing Mix. Use this mixture to
dress the eggplant.

Pickled *Daikon* Radish with *Zha-cai*
(*Daikon no zha-zai zuke*)

Makes 4 servings
200 g/7 oz *daikon* radish, 50g/2 oz *zha-cai*

1 Peel *daikon* radish and cut into fine matchsticks.
2 Wash *zha-cai* (preserved vegetables). Cut as
with the *daikon* radish.
3 Mix *daikon* radish and *zha-cai* by rubbing them
lightly together. Let stand for 20–30 minutes,
allowing the saltiness of the *zha-cai* to flavor the
daikon. Before serving, drain off excess water.

Pickled Cucumber in Soy Sauce
(*Kyuri no shoyu zuke*)

Makes 4 servings

2 cucumbers, 4 radishes
Seasonings: 2 tbsp soy sauce, 1 tbsp rice vinegar, 1 tsp sugar, 2 tbsp sesame oil

1 Beat cucumbers with a wooden pestle until they crack open. Break into bite-sized pieces. Prepare radishes the same.
2 Mix Seasonings. and add to the vegetables and let stand for 20 minutes, stirring occasionally.

Pickled Turnips Flavored with Seaweed
(*Kabu no kobucha zuke*)

Makes 4 servings

4 turnips, 100 g/3¼ oz turnip tops (greens)
Seasoning: 1 tbsp powdered *konbu* seaweed tea (*kobucha*)

1 Peel turnips, cut lengthwise in half, then slice thinly. Boil turnip greens and cut into 3 cm/1 inch lengths.
2 Season with powdered *konbu* seaweed tea, rubbing the powder into the turnips with your hands. Let stand for 10–15 minutes to allow the flavors to combine.

Pickled Cabbage Flavored with *Yukari*
(*Kyabetsu no yukari zuke*)

Makes 4 servings

400 g/13 oz cabbage, 1 tsp salt
Seasoning: 1 tbsp powdered *yukari*

1 Thinly slice cabbage. Sprinkle with salt and toss. Squeeze out the water released from the cabbage.
2 Add powdered *yukari* and toss. Let stand for 10 minutes to allow the flavors to combine.

Western-Style Rice Dishes

A Western dish such as beef stroganoff, ratatouille, or hamburger served alongside rice on one plate makes for a satisfying meal. *Hayashi* Rice and Chicken Rice are commonly found on the menus of Western-style restaurants throughout Japan.

Seafood Cooked in Cream Sauce with Rice

Paprika gives this cream sauce its beautiful color. The rice is molded and served in a decorative shape.

Makes 4 servings

2 rice cooker cups of rice, cooked
3 tablespoons minced parsley
2 tablespoons butter
16 prawns (black tiger)
200 g/3¼ oz squid rings
¼ teaspoon salt
Dash of pepper
½ onion (80 g/3 oz)
2 sweet red peppers
1 tablespoon salad oil
⅓ cup white wine
½ tablespoon paprika
Broth A:
  ½ chicken bouillon cube, dissolved in
    ⅔ cup hot water
1 teaspoon salt
Dash of pepper
1½ cups fresh cream

1 Peel and devein the prawns. Peel the skin off the squid and cut into 1 cm/½ inch rings. Season both with salt and pepper.
2 Thinly slice the onion into rings. Remove the seeds and cut the sweet red pepper into 1 cm/½ inch rings. (Picture 1)
3 Heat a heavy pan and add salad oil. Sauté the onions until translucent. Add the sweet red pepper and quickly sauté. Add the prawns and squid and sauté until the prawns are pink and the squid form ring shapes. (Picture 2)
4 Add white wine and bring to a boil. Add paprika and Broth A. Add salt and pepper and bring to a boil again. Add fresh cream and lower the heat. Continue cooking for 2–3 minutes longer. (Pictures 3–5)
5 Mix the minced parsley and butter with freshly cooked rice. Mold the rice into a 10 cm/4 inch-wide patty about 3–4 cm/1¼ inch thick. Place the molded rice on individual serving plates next to the seafood in its sauce.
(Picture 6)

Beef Stroganoff with Rice

This Russian dish of beef cooked in sour cream goes well with rice.

Makes 4 servings
2 rice cooker cups of rice, cooked
  2 tablespoons butter
  1 teaspoon salt
  Dash of pepper
300 g/10 oz thinly sliced beef
  ¼ teaspoon salt
  Dash of pepper
1 large onion (200 g/7 oz)
1 clove garlic
100 g/3½ oz button mushrooms
3 tablespoons butter
1 tablespoon brandy
1 tablespoon flour
1 tablespoon paprika
Broth A:
  1½ cups tomato purée
  1¼ teaspoons salt
  A dash of pepper
  1 beef bouillon cube
  2 cups water
  1 bay leaf
½ cup sour cream
Italian parsley

1 Cut the beef into 1 cm/½ inch strips. Season with salt and pepper.

2 Cut the onion lengthwise and slice thinly. Crush the clove of garlic with a knife. Thinly slice the mushrooms.

3 Melt the butter in a heavy bottomed pot. Sauté the garlic to season the butter, then remove the garlic. Add the onions and cook until soft. Stir in the mushrooms and quickly sauté. Add the beef and sauté until slightly browned.

4 Drizzle brandy over the meat, then sprinkle in flour and paprika. Stir well and cook a little longer. Add Broth A and stir constantly from the bottom of the pot until it comes to a boil. Then reduce the heat and cook for an additional 20 minutes. Occasionally skim the scum off the surface.

5 Turn the heat off. Gently blend in the sour cream.

6 Mix the butter, salt and pepper with freshly prepared rice. If possible, use a circular mold for each serving of rice and place molded rice on individual plates. Ladle beef stroganoff over the rice. Garnish with sprigs of parsley.

Ratatouille with Rice

This stew is chock-full of vegetables.

Makes 4 servings
2 rice cooker cups of rice, cooked
6 slices bacon (100 g/3¼ oz)
1 onion (150 g/5 oz)
3 eggplants (250 g/8¼ oz)
1 zucchini (200 g/7 oz)
3 green peppers
1 clove garlic
3 tablespoons salad oil
2 cans stewed tomatoes (about 800 g/1⅔ lb)
1 slightly rounded teaspoon salt
1 bouquet garni
Dash of pepper
Sprig of fresh basil

1 Cut the bacon into 2–3 cm/1 inch pieces.
2 Dice the onion into 2 cm/½ inch cubes. Peel and slice the eggplants into 1 cm/½ inch rounds. Slice the zucchini into 1 cm/½ inch rounds. Remove the seeds from the green pepper and dice into 1 cm/½ inch cubes. Mince the garlic.
3 Heat a heavy pot and add the salad oil. Sauté the garlic; then add onion and sauté until translucent.
4 Add the bacon, eggplant, green pepper and zucchini and sauté in that order until liquid has evaporated.
5 Squeeze the tomatoes to break them up. Add the tomatoes and their liquid to the pot. Add the salt, pepper and bouquet garni. Cover the pot and cook over low heat for 20–30 minutes, stirring occasionally. The vegetables should be soft and the liquid should be thick.
6 Divide the rice among four serving dishes and place equal portions of ratatouille atop the rice. Garnish with fresh basil leaves.

Beef Stew in Demiglace Sauce with Rice
(*Hayashi raisu*)

One of the first Western dishes in Japan, this stew still captures the hearts of Japanese.

Makes 4 servings
2 rice cooker cups of rice, cooked
300 g/10 oz beef, thinly sliced and in
    small pieces
2 onions (300 g/10 oz)
1 can mushrooms (200 g/7 oz)
1 clove garlic, minced
3 tablespoons butter
Seasoning Mix A:
    ½ tablespoon sugar
    ¼ teaspoon salt
    Dash of black pepper
2½ tablespoons flour
Sauce:
    2 tablespoons red wine or saké
    ⅔ cup tomato purée
    1 beef bouillon cube
    1 cup hot water
    2 bay leaves
1 can demiglace sauce (280 g/9⅓ oz)
⅔ teaspoon salt
Dash of black pepper
Dill pickles

1 Slice the onion into 7–8 mm/⅓ inch-thick pieces. Cut the mushrooms in half lengthwise.
2 Melt the butter in a heavy pot and sauté the garlic and onion. When the onion becomes transparent, add the mushrooms and sauté a little longer. Add the beef and sauté until cooked.
3 Add Seasoning Mix A to the meat and sauté. Add flour and cook until the flour is well mixed. Add the sauce ingredients and bring to a boil. Turn down the heat and cook for 20 minutes, stirring occasinally from the bottom.
4 Add the demiglace sauce, salt and pepper and cook for another 10–15 minutes.
5 Place the rice to one side of shallow individual serving dishes. Ladle the beef stew on the other side. Garnish with small slices of dill pickles.

Hamburger with Rice

Hamburger patties cooked in sauce are garnished with french fried potatoes.

Makes 4 servings
2 rice cooker cups of rice, cooked
4 cooked hamburger patties, see page 126
2 tablespoons saké
2 green peppers
2 sweet red peppers
4 fresh *shiitake* mushrooms
½ tablespoon salad oil
Broth A:
  ½ beef bouillon cube, dissolved in
    ½ cup hot water
1 can demiglace sauce (280 g/8⅔ oz)
300 g/10 oz spinach
½ tablespoon salad oil
Dash of salt
Dash of pepper
100 g/3¼ oz french fried potatoes

1 Remove the seeds from the green and red peppers and then slice lengthwise into 1 cm/½ inch pieces. Remove the stems from the mushrooms and slice into 1 cm/½ inch pieces. Boil the spinach for a short time and then plunge into cold water to cool. Squeeze to remove excess water and then cut into 3–4 cm/1¼ inch lengths.
2 Heat the frying pan and add ½ tablespoon of salad oil. Sauté the spinach quickly with salt and pepper. Put aside.
3 Heat the pan and add ½ tablespoon of salad oil. Sauté peppers and mushrooms. Add Broth A, then add demiglace sauce. Bring to a boil and continue cooking over low heat for 1–2 minutes.
4 Add the cooked hamburgers to the pan and cook for 2–3 minutes longer.
5 Divide the rice among four individual serving dishes and place the hamburgers on top of the rice. Pour the sauce over the hamburgers. Garnish with french fried potatoes and spinach.

Chicken Rice

Japanese people still crave this dish, a childhood staple, even after they've grown up.

Makes 4 servings
2 rice cooker cups of rice, cooked
200 g/ 7 oz chicken breast
   ⅕ teaspoon salt
   Dash of pepper
1 onion
⅓ cup green peas (frozen)
2 tablespoons salad oil
2 tablespoons butter
⅓ cup ketchup
1⅓ teaspoons salt
Dash of pepper

1 Cut the chicken into 1.5 cm/½ inch cubes. Toss with salt and pepper.
2 Dice the onion into 1 cm/½ inch cubes. Place the green peas in a colander and pour boiling water over them.
3 Sauté the chicken in salad oil until cooked. Add onion and sauté until translucent.
4 Add the butter and rice (if the rice is completely cold, reheat cold rice in a microwave oven, so it separates.) Cook until the rice is no longer sticky.
5 Add ketchup, salt and pepper and quickly sauté until the flavors are well mingled. At the last minute, sprinkle with green peas and serve.

* Use a Chinese wok to cook 4 servings together, or cook 2 servings at a time in a smaller frying pan.

Crab Doria (*Kani iri doria*)

A rice gratin topped with plenty of white sauce.

Makes 4 servings
750 g/1⅔ lb cooked rice
200 g/7 oz canned crab meat
100 g/3⅓ oz cuttlefish or squid
  4 tablespoons white wine
½ onion
50 g/1⅔ oz mushrooms
2 tablespoons butter
2 tablespoons ketchup
⅔ teaspoon salt
Dash of pepper
White sauce:
  2 tablespoons butter
  3 tablespoons flour
  3 cups milk
  ⅓ teaspoon salt
  Dash of pepper
  1 bay leaf
Some butter
Parmesan cheese

1 Break the crab meat into flakes and remove any soft bones. Cut the cuttlefish into 1 cm1/1½ inch-square pieces. Thinly slice the onion and mushrooms.

2 Place the cuttlefish in a pot. Drizzle with white wine and sprinkle with salt and pepper. Cover the pot and quickly steam.

3 To prepare the white sauce, combine the butter, flour, milk, salt, pepper and bay leaf in a pot and place over low heat.

4 Melt butter in a frying pan. Sauté the sliced onion and then the mushrooms. Add the rice and continue to sauté. Mix in the cuttlefish and crab meat and season with ketchup, salt and pepper.

5 Rub butter over the inside of individual oven-proof serving dishes and fill with the rice mixture. Cover the surface of the mixture with white sauce. Sprinkle with parmesan cheese to taste before placing in an oven which has been pre-heated to 220°C/425°F. Cook in the oven for 10–15 minutes until the surface browns.

Rice Croquette (*Raisu Korokke*)

Minced beef and tomato-flavored rice are combined and formed into oval patties, which are then coated in bread crumbs and deep-fried.

Makes 4 servings
500 g/5 oz cooked rice
150 g/5 oz minced beef
½ onion (70–80 g/2⅓-2⅔ oz)
1 clove garlic
2 tablespoons flour
1 tablespoon salad oil
1 tablespoon butter
¼ cup red wine
400 g/1⅓ oz canned tomatoes, cooked in water
2 tablespoons ketchup
½ teaspoon salt (or more)
Dash of pepper
Coating for croquettes:
  Flour and beaten egg
  Bread crumbs

Oil for deep-frying
½–1 lemon

1 Mince the onion and garlic.
2 Heat the butter and salad oil in a pot. Sauté the minced onion and garlic. Add the minced beef and flour, and continue to sauté.
3 Add the red wine, canned tomatoes, ketchup, salt and pepper. Continue to cook for about 20 minutes. Set the mixture aside to cool.
4 Combine the rice with the mixture and divide and shape into 8 oval patties. Cover each patty lightly with flour, dunk in the beaten egg, and then coat with the bread crumbs.
5 Place the croquettes in oil which has been heated to 180°C/360°F. Deep-fry quickly. Squeeze fresh lemon juice over the freshly prepared croquettes and serve immediately. Garnish with readily available fresh vegetables, such as lettuce and tomatoes.

Small Salads

Because rice often accounts for much of the volume,
these dishes are often lacking in vegetables.
Balance out the meal by serving a salad as a side dish.

Mushroom Salad
(*Kinoko sarada*)

Makes 4 servings
8 fresh *shiitake*, 1 bunch *shimeji* mushrooms
Dressing: 2 tbsp salad oil, 2 tbsp white wine, 1 tbsp
rice vinegar, ¼ tsp salt, a dash of pepper
Garnish: chopped parsley

1 Remove the stems from *shiitake* mushrooms
and then cut in half. Break apart *shimeji* mushrooms.
2 Quickly sauté the *shiitake* and *shimeji* mushrooms in salad oil, then drizzle in white wine.
When the mushrooms have softened, add rice
vinegar, salt and pepper. Sprinkle chopped parsley
over the mushrooms.

Onion and Watercress Salad
(*Tamanegi to kureson no sarada*)

Makes 4 servings
½ small onion, 1 bunch watercress, 3 slices ham
Dressing Mix: 1 tbsp rice vinegar, 2 tbsp salad oil,
a pinch of salt, a dash of pepper

1 Thinly slice onion into rings. Remove and discard the stems from watercress. Chill the onions
and watercress in cold water, then dry well. Cut
ham slices into thin strips.
2 Mix together Dressing Mix. Toss with the
onions, watercress and ham.

Cucumber Yogurt Salad
(*Kyuri no yoguruto sarada*)

Makes 4 servings

3 cucmbers, ½ tsp salt

Dressing Mix: ½ cup plain yogurt, 1tbsp rice vinegar, 2 tbsp salad oil, ⅓ tsp salt, a dash of pepper

1 Thinly slice 3 cucumbers and sprinkle with salt to remove excess water. Wash the cucumbers and squeeze dry.

2 In a bowl, beat together the Dressing Mix. Add the cucumbers and toss.

Celery and Apple Salad
(*Serori to ringo no sarada*)

Makes 4 servings

1 stalk celery, a dash of salt, 1 apple

Dressing Mix: 2 tbsp yogurt, 3 tbsp mayonnaise, ⅓ tbsp lemon juice

1 Remove and discard the fibrous veins in the stalk of celery and cut into 3 mm/⅛ inch slices. Sprinkle with salt to remove excess water. Squeeze dry. Cut apple into 3 mm/⅛ inch triangular slices.

2 Mix together Dressing Mix and toss with celery and apple.

Green Onion and Fish Cake Salad with Plum Paste
(*Negi to kamaboko no ume sarada*)

Makes 4 servings

1 bunch green onions, 100 g/3¼ oz fish cake (*kamaboko*)

Paste Mix: ½ tbsp plum paste, ½ tbsp rice vinegar, 1 tbsp salad oil.

1 Cut green onions into 3–4 cm/1¼ inch lengths. Cut fish cake into small bite-sized pieces.

2 Combine Paste Mix and toss with green onions and fish cake.

Hot and Spicy Ethnic Food

Various ethnic rice dishes are featured in this section: Indian and Thai curries, Korean *bibimba*, spicy Chinese fried rice, as well as other dishes featuring the flavors of Southeast Asia.

Thai-Style Green Curry
(*Taifu gurin kare*)

This chicken curry is made with green curry paste and coconut milk, both of which are readily available.

Makes 6 servings
Cooked rice (made from 3 rice cooker cups
   of Thai rice)
300 g/⅔ lb chicken thighs
100 g/3⅓ oz boiled bamboo shoots
2 Asian eggplants
1 packet green curry paste (50 g/1⅔ oz)
1 tablespoon salad oil
1 can coconut milk (about 400 cc/13⅓ oz)
Seasoning Mixture:
   2 tablespoons *namplaa* fish sauce
   1 tablespoon sugar
   Dash of powdered cumin
   Some fresh coriander
   1½ cups water
10 small chilli peppers
3–4 sprigs basil

1 Cut the chicken into 3 cm/2¼ inch cubes and cut the bamboo shoots into 3 cm/2¼ inch-long slices. Peel the eggplants and cut into bite-sized pieces. Soak the eggplant in water, then drain and pat dry. (Picture 1)
2 Heat the salad oil in a pot. Add the curry paste and sauté over medium heat. Add the chicken cubes and continue to cook until the color of the meat changes. Add the coconut milk little by little while stirring. (Pictures 2–4)
3 Add the seasoning mixture, bamboo shoots and eggplant. Bring to a boil, then turn down the heat to low. Continue to cook for another 15 minutes. (Picture 5)
4 Remove and discard the stems of the chilli peppers and add them to the pot. Tear the basil into smaller pieces and add to the mixture. Continue to cook for 1–2 minutes longer on low heat, then turn off the heat. (Picture 6)
5 Place warm rice in individual serving dishes. Place a serving of curry next to the rice. Tear the fresh coriander and mix with curry, if desired.

Curry Rice

Pork curry with some special ingredients—heaps of apples and vegetables.

Makes 4 servings
2 rice cooker cups of rice, cooked
500 g/1¼ lb cubed pork
  ⅓ teaspoon salt
  Dash of pepper
1 clove garlic
1 piece ginger
1 carrot (150 g/5 oz)
1 onion (150 g/5 oz)
1 stalk celery (100 g/3¼ oz)
1 apple (150 g/5 oz)
4 tablespoons salad oil
4 tablespoons curry powder
4 tablespoons flour
Seasoning Mix A:
  3 tablespoons ketchup
  1 tablespoon soy sauce
  Heaping teaspoon of salt
  Dash of pepper
  3 beef bouillon cubes
  3 cups hot water
1–2 tablespoons garam masala
30 g/1 oz raisins

1 Season the pork with salt and pepper.
2 Peel the ginger, garlic and carrot and then grate separately. Peel the onion, celery and apple and then mince separately. (Picture 1)
3 Heat up a heavy pot and add 2 tablespoons of salad oil. Brown the pork well, then remove it from the pot. (Picture 2)
4 Add the remaining 2 tablespoons of salad oil to the pot. Add in order: ginger, garlic, onion, carrot, celery and apple and sauté for 15–20 minutes until dry. (Picture 3)
5 Add the pork. Then add curry powder and flour separately and sauté well until the flavors are released. (Picture 4)
6 Add Seasoning Mix A and stir constantly from the bottom of the pot until the mixture comes to a boil. Reduce the heat and cook for 40 minutes to one hour. Occasionally skim the scum off the surface.
7 Add garam masala and cook for another 4–5 minutes. (Picture 5)
8 Wash the raisins with warm water and mix into freshly prepared rice. Place the rice on one side of individual serving dishes and place the curry on the other side.

Dry Curry

In this dish, the curry is cooked until it's very dry and then it is mixed with pilaf.

Makes 4–6 servings
Pilaf:
    3 cups rice
    3 cups water or soup stock
    1⅓ tablespoons butter
    4 tablespoons chopped parsley
300 g/⅔ lb minced beef
1 large onion (200 g/7 oz)
1 carrot
1 clove garlic
1 piece fresh ginger root
4 tablespoons curry powder
2½ cups soup stock
3 tablespoons ketchup
3 tablespoons butter
⅔ teaspoon salt
Dash of pepper
60 g/2 oz raisins

1 To prepare the pilaf, place the rice (which has been well washed) in a pot or rice cooker with the butter and the appropriate amount of water (or soup stock). Cook the rice in the usual way for ordinary rice. Let stand for a short time after it has finished cooking, and then mix the rice with the chopped parsley. (Picture 1)

2 Mince the onion, carrot, garlic and ginger.

3 Melt 3 tablespoons of butter in a pot. Add the garlic, ginger and onion. Cook until the onions have browned. Add the carrot and minced beef. Continue cooking while separating the beef. (Pictures 2–3)

4 When the beef has browned, add the curry powder and continue to cook for 1 minute. Add the soup stock, ketchup, salt and pepper. Continue to cook for 15–20 minutes. When all the liquid has evaporated, add the raisins and cook for just a short time longer. (Pictures 4–6)

5 Place the pilaf with parsley in serving dishes and serve with the desired amount of dry curry alongside. Mix as you eat.

Korean-Style *Donburi* (*Bibimba*)

Spicy beef and vegetables over rice prepared
Korean style.

Makes 4 servings
2 rice cooker cups of rice, cooked
150 g/5 oz bracken, reconstituted if dried
   (*zenmai*)
  ½ green onion, minced
  Minced garlic
  1 tablespoon sesame oil

Seasoning Mix A:
  3 tablespoons soy sauce
  ½ tablespoon chopped white sesame seeds
  Dash of red pepper
200 g/7 oz soy bean sprouts
  1 medium green onion, minced
  ½ tablespoon sesame oil
  1 teaspoon chopped white sesame seeds
1 carrot (about 150 g/5 oz)
Seasoning Mix B:

⅓ teaspoon salt
1 teaspoon sesame oil
½ teaspoon soy sauce
½ green onion, minced
1 teaspoon chopped white sesame seeds
Dash of powdered red chili pepper
200 g/7 oz spinach
Seasoning Mix C:
⅓ teaspoon salt
Dash of pepper
½ tablespoon soy sauce
1 teaspoon sesame oil
1 teaspoon toasted and chopped white
   sesame seeds
3 cucumbers
1 teaspoon salt
1 tablespoon sesame oil
Ingredients D:
½ green onion, minced
1 teaspoon toasted and chopped white
   sesame seeds
2 eggs
⅛ teaspoon salt
1 teaspoon salad oil
200 g/7 oz thinly sliced beef
Ingredients E:
1 teaspoon sugar
2 tablespoons soy sauce
1 tablespoon sesame oil
Dash of pepper
1 teaspoon grated garlic
5 cm/2 inch green onion, minced
2 tablespoons chopped white sesame seeds
½ tablespoon salad oil
Korean hot soybean paste (*kochujang*)

1 For this dish, you must prepare five separate vegetable mixtures. To prepare the first, cut the bracken into 4–5 cm/2 inch lengths. Sauté the green onions, garlic and bracken in sesame oil. Add Seasoning Mix A and continue cooking until dry.

2 Remove and discard the bean part of the bean sprouts. Quickly boil the sprouts in salted water (1 teaspoon of salt to 1 cup of water), then drain in a colander. Sauté the green onions and bean sprouts in sesame oil. Sprinkle sesame seeds over the mixture.

3 Cut the carrot into 4–5 cm/2 inch-long match sticks. Quickly boil and then drain in a colander. Mix in Seasoning Mix B while the carrot is still hot.

4 Boil the spinach until it turns bright green. Plunge into cold water. When the spinach has cooled, squeeze out the excess water and cut into 5 cm/2 inch lengths. Mix with Seasoning Mix C.

5 Thinly slice the cucumbers, and rub in salt to remove excess water. Quickly sauté in sesame oil and then add Ingredients D.

6 To make the egg strips: First stir the eggs and add salt. Put salad oil in a frying pan. Prepare two very thin crêpe-like omelets. Remove from the pan and cut into strips 5 cm x 5 mm/2 inch x ¼ inch.

7 Place the thinly sliced beef in a bowl with Ingredients E and mix lightly. Let stand for 15–20 minutes. Quickly fry the beef in ½ tablespoon salad oil. Remove from the frying pan and cut into 3 cm/1 inch-long pieces.

(Picture 1–2)

8 Divide the warm rice among four deep individual serving bowls (*donburi*) and arrange the vegetable mixtures in a circle on top. Place the beef in the center. At the table, allow each person to add *kochujang* according to taste. Each person must mix everything in his or her own bowl together before eating.

(Picture 3)

Tropical Fried Rice (*Toropikaru chahan*)

Seasoned with fish sauce and garnished with slices of fresh fruit, this dish is a refreshing version of the more traditional type of *chahan*.

Makes 4 servings
2 rice cooker cups of rice, cooked
120 g/4 oz thinly sliced pork
⅛ teaspoon salt
Dash of pepper
2 tablespoons dried shrimp
½ red onion
1 red sweet pepper
3 tablespoons salad oil
2 tablespoons (or more) *nampulaa* fish sauce
Dash of salt
Dash of pepper
1 small papaya
2 kiwis
1 lime or lemon
Sprigs of fresh coriander

1 Cut the pork into 1 cm/½ inch pieces, then season with salt and pepper.

2 Soak the dried shrimp in warm water for fifteen minutes to reconstitute. Then drain and pat dry. Chop the red onion into small pieces. Remove the seeds from the sweet pepper and dice into 1 cm cubes.

3 Heat a Chinese wok and add salad oil. Stir-fry the pork over high heat until cooked. Add the shrimp, red onion and sweet red pepper.

4 Add rice and reduce the heat to medium. Continue to stir-fry until the rice is no longer sticky. Season with *nampulaa* fish sauce, salt and pepper.

5 Divide the fried rice among four individual serving plates. Decorate with small slices of papaya and kiwi and garnish with coriander leaves and lime wedges. Squeeze some lime juice over the rice before eating.

106

Rice Mixed with Stir-Fried Beef and *Kimchee*
(*Gyuniku to kimuchi itame no maze-gohan*)

The liquid from the *kimchee* will also add a touch of flavor to this dish.

Makes 4 servings
2 rice cooker cups of rice, cooked
100 g/3½ oz thinly sliced beef
170 g/6 oz *kimchee* (Korean pickled cabbage)
80 g/2⅔ oz Chinese scallions
1 tablespoon sesame oil
Seasoning Mix A:
  1 tablespoon saké
  ½ tablespoon sugar
  1 tablespoon soy sauce
1 tablespoon toasted white sesame seeds

1 Cut the beef into 2 cm/1 inch-long pieces.
2 Squeeze the *kimchee* to remove its liquid. Reserve. Cut the *kimchee* into 1 cm/½ inch-long pieces. Cut the scallions into 2 cm/⅔ inch lengths.
3 Heat a frying pan and add the sesame oil. Stir-fry the beef until cooked. Add *kimchee* and then the scallions and stir-fry quickly. Add Seasoning Mix A and continue to stir-fry for a short time longer.
4 After the rice has finished cooking, mix the rice well from the bottom. Then add the beef and *kimchee* mixture and the reserved *kimchee* liquid to the freshly cooked rice and mix well.
5 Divide the rice mixture into four individual serving dishes and sprinkle with sesame seeds.

Prawns with Chilli Sauce Over Rice
(*Ebi chiri-don*)

This dish features the ever-popular chilli sauce over rice.

Makes 4 servings
2 rice cooker cups of rice, cooked
400 g/13 oz prawns
1 tablespoon saké
1 tablespoon *katakuriko* or cornstarch
Salt / Salad oil
80 g/3 oz green beans
½ green onion
1 clove garlic
1 piece ginger
1 tablespoon salad oil
Seasoning Mix A:
   1 tablespoon soy sauce
   1 tablespoon Chinese brown bean paste
   (*dou-pan-chiang*)
   6 tablespoons ketchup
   ⅛ teaspoon salt
Broth B:
   1⅔ cups hot water
   1 chicken bouillon cube
1½ tablespoons *katakuriko* or cornstarch,
   dissolved in 3 tablespoons water

1 Remove the heads, tails and shells from prawns and devein. Wash in lightly salted water and dry well. Coat with saké and *katakuriko*. Add salt and a little salad oil to boiling water. Add the prawns to the water separetely, so that they don't stick together. Boil for a short time, until they turn pink. Let drain in a colander.
2 Snap off the ends of the green beans and remove the strings. Cut into 3–4 cm/1⅔ inch lengths and boil until they turn bright green. Drain in a colander.
3 Mince the green onion, ginger and garlic.
4 Heat a frying pan, then add 1 tablespoon salad oil. Stir-fry the green onions, ginger and garlic. Add Seasoning Mix A and bring to a boil over high heat. Then add Broth B. Let the mixture return to a boil. Add the prawns and green beans and return to a boil. Add the dissolved *katakuriko*. Stir until the sauce has thickened.
5 Divide the rice among four deep individual serving bowls (*donburi*) and place equal amounts of the prawns and sauce over the rice.

Chinese-Style Beef and *Miso* Over Rice
(*Chukafu niku miso-don*)

Add spicy Chinese *miso* to this dish to make it as hot as you like.

Makes 4 servings
2 rice cooker cups of rice, cooked
250 g/8 oz ground pork
  ½ tablespoon saké
  ½ tablespoon soy sauce
  1 teaspoon ginger juice
4 dried *shiitake* mushrooms
70 g/2½ oz boiled bamboo shoots
½ green onion
2 tablespoons salad oil
Seasoning Mix A:
  2 tablespoons red *miso*
  1 tablespoon sugar
  1 tablespoon saké
  1 tablespoon soy sauce
  1 tablespoon water
2 cucumbers
1 tablespoon Chinese brown bean paste
  (*dou-pan-chiang*)

1 Add the soy sauce, saké and ginger juice to ground pork. Mix well.
2 Soak the dried *shiitake* mushrooms in water to cover until they become plump. Remove the stems and mince the *shiitake* and bamboo shoots into 5 mm/¼ inch cubes.
3 Mince the green onion.
4 Heat the salad oil in a Chinese wok or frying pan and add the ground pork. Cook until the pork pieces separate. Then add the *shiitake* mushrooms and bamboo shoots and sauté a little longer.
5 Add the minced green onion and Seasoning Mix A. Sauté until all of the ingredients are well-coated and shiny.
6 Thinly slice the cucumbers at a diagonal and then julienne.
7 Divide the rice among four deep individual serving bowls (*donburi*). Top each with equal amounts of the pork mixture. Garnish with sliced cucumber. Serve with brown bean paste on the side, so that each person can season this dish to his or her own taste.

Ethnic-Style Desserts

After a hot and spicy ethnic dish,
a sweet and refreshing dessert with plenty of fruit cleanses your palate.

Coconut Milk with Fruit and Tapioca
(*Furutsu to tapioka iri kokonattsu miruku*)

1 cup coconut milk, ½ cup milk, ½ cup sugar, a dash of salt, ⅓ cup tapioca
16 lychee nuts, 12-16 strawberries

1 Combine coconut milk and 2½ cups of water. Add milk and mix. Stir in sugar, salt and tapioca. Let the mixture stand for 3–4 minutes.
2 Heat the pot while mixing well from the bottom with a wooden spoon, until the tapioca becomes translucent. Turn off the heat and let the pot cool down a little bit. Refrigerate.
3 Remove and discard the skin and seeds from lychee nuts. Cut strawberries into halves or quarters. Place the coconut milk mixture in serving dishes and garnish with the lychee nuts and strawberries.

Mint Jelly with Melon Balls
(*Minto zeri no meron zoe*)

2 packets powdered agar-agar, ⅓ cup peppermint leaves, 5 g/⅙ oz fresh mint leaves, ⅔ cup sugar, 1 melon spooned out into balls

1 Place powdered agar-agar and 3 cups of water into a pot and dissolve over medium heat. Sieve mixture and then add peppermint leaves. Pour the mixture into a deep container and refrigerate until it sets.
2 Add fresh mint leaves to 2½ cups of water and heat until the aroma of the mint is released. Add sugar. When the sugar has dissolved, let the mixture cool and sieve. Refrigerate.
3 Spoon out a portion of mint jelly and place in a serving dish. Pour the syrup over the jelly. Garnish each serving with melon balls.

Banana Fritter
(*Banana no furitta*)

Batter Mix: 80 g/2⅔ oz flour, Dash of salt, 1 egg yolk, ⅓ cup milk, ½ tsps butter
4 bananas peeled and cut each into 2-3 pieces, lemon juice, egg white, 1 tbsp sugar, powdered sugar

1 Sprinkle lemon juice over the bananas.
2 Beat egg white into stiff peaks. Add sugar and continue to beat. Fold into the batter.
3 Coat the bananas with the batter. Deep-fry. Place in serving dishes. Sprinkle with powdered sugar to taste.

Junket with Watermelon
(*Annin dofu no suika zoe*)

1 packet powdered agar-agar, 1 tsp gelatin powder; dissolved in 2 tbsp water, 4 tbsp sugar, Dash of almond extract, ½ cup milk, ½ cup fresh cream, 4 tbsp sugar
300 g/10 oz of watermelon; cut into cubes

1 Dissolve powered agar-agar in 1½ cups of boiling water. Mix gelatin, sugar, and almond extract with agar-agar mixture. When the mixture has cooled, stir in milk and cream. Sieve. Place in four individual serving dishes. Chill in the refrigerator.
2 Dissolve sugar in 1 cup of water to make the syrup. Chill. Pour the syrup over the junket. Place watermelon over the junket.

Agar-Agar with Kiwi Fruit
(*Kiwi no kanten yose*)

5 g/⅕ oz agar-agar; 2½ cups water, 80 g/3 oz sugar, juice of ½ lemon
1 kiwi fruit; cut into 5 mm/½ inch slices

1 Place water and agar-agar in a pot and bring to a boil, then add sugar. Cook 4–5 minutes over low heat. Allow the mixture to cool down, and then stir in lemon juice.
2 When the agar-agar mixture is set, pour it into a mold. Add kiwi slices into the mold and refrigerate completely. Slice and serve

Soup *Gohan*, Soupy Rice Dishes

Rice porridge is prepared by boiling cooked rice, vegetables and seafood together in a soup. Rice gruel uses more liquid and the white rice is cooked until it becomes very soft. In China, rice gruel is an essential part of breakfast.

Asari Clams in Rice Porridge
(*Asari zosui*)

A rice dish in which cooked rice is quickly boiled with Japanese soup stock is referred to as *zosui*. The addition of littleneck clams will make this dish more flavourful.

Makes 4–6 servings
500 g/1 lb cooked rice
400 g/1 lb *asari* clams
Salted water:
   3 cups of water
   1 tablespoon salt
4 cups water or *dashi* stock
1½ teaspoons salt
2 teaspoons soy sauce
6–7 chives

1 Soak the *asari* clams in a bowl of salted water for 5–6 hours to wash away sand. When washing, rub the clam shells together. Place them in a colander to drain. (Pictutes 1–2)
2 Place the cooked rice in a colander and wash quickly with water to remove stickiness. Then set aside to drain. (Picture 3)
3 In a pot, bring water or *dashi* to a boil. Season with salt and soy sauce. Add the littleneck clams. When it returns to a boil, turn down the heat to medium. (Pictures 4–6)
4 When the clams begin to open, quickly stir in the cooked rice. Bring to a boil and let it cook for 1–2 minutes. Turn the heat off. Chop the chives into 5 mm/¼ inch-long pieces and sprinkle over the dish.

Crab Meat in Rice Porridge (*Kani zosui*)

A very sophisticated flavor is created with crab meat and the final touch – egg flowers.

Makes 4–6 servings
500 g/1 lb cooked rice
100 g/3⅓ oz crab meat
5 cups *dashi* stock
1½ teaspoons salt
1 tablespoon soy sauce
20 g/⅓ oz trefoil (*mitsuba*)
4 eggs, beaten

1 Place the cooked rice in a colander and wash quickly with water to remove stickiness. Then set aside to drain.
2 Remove any soft bones or cartilage from the crab meat and break into bite-sized pieces.
3 In a pot, bring the *dashi* to a boil. Season with salt and soy sauce. Add the rice. When it returns to a boil, turn down the heat to medium and cook for 1–2 minutes longer. Add the crab meat and quickly stir.
4 Cut the trefoil leaves into 2–3 cm/1 inch-long pieces and sprinkle over the rice mixture. Cover the surface of the rice mixture with the beaten eggs. When the eggs are half-cooked, turn off the heat.

Milk and Rice Porridge (*Gyunyu zosui*)

Enjoy this Western-style vegetable rice porridge as a soup.

Makes 4–6 servings
500 g/1 lb cooked rice
150 g/5 oz onion
150 g/5 oz carrot
120 g/4 oz *shimeji* mushrooms
5 cups water
4 bouillon cubes
2 cups milk
Dash of salt
Dash of pepper
Chopped parsley

1 Cut the onion into 1 cm cubes. Cut the carrot into 5 mm/⅕ inch-thick, 1 cm/⅓ inch squares. Cut the *shimeji* mushrooms off at their base and roughly break apart.

2 Place the vegetables prepared in Step 1 into a pot, together with the water and bouillon cubes, and bring to a boil. Turn the heat down to low and continue to cook until the vegetables are soft.

3 Add the cooked rice to the pot, roughly breaking apart the chunks. Add the milk. As the mixture starts to boil, season with salt and pepper and then turn off the heat.

4 Divide the rice mixture into individual serving bowls and garnish with chopped parsley before serving.

* For variation, add eggs in step 3, after the heat has been turned off. Allow one egg for each person and cook the eggs for as long as desired.

Korean-Style Rice Porridge (*Kankokufu zosui*)

This dish features rich flavors and exciting spices.

Makes 4-6 servings
600 g/1⅔ lb cooked rice
150 g/5 oz thinly sliced beef
50 g/1⅔ oz carrot
40 g/1⅓ oz boiled bamboo shoots
4 fresh *shiitake* mushrooms
10 cm/4 inch piece thick green onion
30 g/1 oz Chinese scallions (*nira*)
1 tablespoons sesame oil
5 cups chicken stock
1½ teaspoons salt
Dash of pepper
1 tablespoon soy sauce
1 tablespoon *kochujang*, Korean soybean paste
1 teaspoon powdered hot chilli pepper
1 teaspoon grated garlic

1 Cut the beef into 2 cm/¾ inch-wide pieces.

2 Cut the carrot into 3 cm/1¼ inch-long strips. Cut the bamboo shoots into similar size strips. Remove and discard the stems of the *shiitake* mushrooms and then cut them into 1 cm/½ inch wide slices.

3 Thinly slice the piece of thick green onion at a diagonal. Cut the Chinese scallions into 4 cm/1½ inch long pieces.

4 Heat the sesame oil in a pot and sauté the beef. When the outside of the meat has cooked, add the carrot, bamboo shoots, *shiitake* mushrooms (in that order) and continue to sauté for a short time longer. Add the chicken stock.

(Pictures 1–3)

5 When the mixture reaches a boil, season with the salt, pepper, soy sauce, *kochujang*, powdered hot chilli pepper and grated garlic. Continue to cook for 3–4 minutes over low heat.

(Picture 4)

6 Mix in the rice. After the mixture has returned to a boil, continue to cook for 1–2 minutes longer. Then sprinkle the chopped green onions and Chinese scallions over the rice mixture.

(Picture 5)

Chinese Rice Porridge (*Chugoku gayu*)

Chinese rice gruel, or *zhou* refers to rice which has been cooked with more water than usual. For *zhou*, add your favorite accompaniments and enjoy with simple dishes.

Makes 4–6 servings
1 cup uncooked rice
1 piece chicken breast (about 250 g/8 oz)
10 cm/4 inch piece green onion
1 piece fresh ginger (15–20 g/⅔ oz)
12–13 cups water
Dash of salt, optional

1 Wash the rice and let it drain well in a colander.   (Picture 1)
2 Quickly rinse the chicken breast. Press down on the piece of green onion and the ginger with the flat side of a knife so that they will release more flavor when cooked.
3 Place the rice, chicken, green onion and ginger in a heavy pot. Add 12–13 cups of water. Place the pot over high heat, stirring occasionally as it reaches a boil.   (Pictures 2–3)
4 When the mixture reaches a boil, turn down the heat to medium-low and continue to slowly

cook for 50–60 minutes. Season with salt, if desired. Remove the chicken, onion and ginger. (If you wish, tear the chicken into small pieces to mix with the gruel). (Picture 4)

Accompaniments to Chinese Rice Gruel

Coriander, fresh:
  Use the leaves and a small amount of stem.
Zha-cai, Chinese salted pickled mustard greens:
  To prepare the *zha-cai*, soak in water for 10 minutes to remove saltiness, then slice.
Pi-tan, Chinese preserved egg
  Peel the egg and cut it lengthwise into 6–8 wedges.
Fu-ru, a special Chinese ingredient
  Fu-ru is a Chinese seasoning made of fermented tofu. Because of its distinct flavor and saltiness, be careful to use only a small amount.
Sliced green onion and ginger
  Cut the green onion julienne-style into 5 cm/2 inch lengths. Peel the ginger and cut into match sticks or thin slices. Soak in cold water to refresh.
Won-ton skins
  Cut into 5 mm/⅕ inch-long strips and quickly deep-fry.

Simple Dishes to Accompany Chinese Rice Gruel

Lettuce with Oyster Sauce:
  In 3 tablespoons of salad oil, quickly stir-fry roughly torn lettuce leaves from one head of lettuce. Add 3 tablespoons saké, 2 tablespoons oyster sauce and ½ tablespoon soy sauce and cook for a short while longer.

Stir-Fried *Daikon* Radish and Dried Shrimp:
  Cut 500 g/1 lb of *daikon* radish into match-

sticks 5 cm/2 inch long by 3 mm/⅛ inch wide. Sprinkle with 1 teaspoon of salt and let stand until the *daikon* radish becomes limp. Soak 4 tablespoons dried shrimp in ½ cup of warm water for 10–15 minutes. Drain and dry well. Chop into small pieces. Heat ½ tablespoon sesame oil and 1 tablespoon salad oil in a frying pan. In the following order, stir-fry the shrimp, ⅓ long piece of chopped green onion, and the *daikon* radish, which has been squeezed dry. Add ⅓ teaspoon of salt, a dash of pepper and 1 tablespoon saké and continue to stir-fry. Sprinkle 1–2 tablespoons of chopped chives over the dish.

Stir-Fried Egg:
  Beat 4 eggs. Add ¼ teaspoon of salt, a dash of pepper and 1 tablespoon of saké and mix well. Heat 3 tablespoons of salad oil in a frying pan. Pour the beaten egg mixture into the pan. As the eggs begin to set, quickly stir with a spatula and then flip them over.

Seafood Risotto

This popular Italian-style rice dish is prepared with plenty of soup and a variety of seafood.

Makes 4 servings
250 g/8⅓ oz rice
¼ onion (40 g/1⅓ oz)
1 clove garlic
1 squid, sac part (100 g/3⅓ oz)
300 g/⅔ lb littleneck clams (*asari*)
Salted water:
  3 cups water
  1 tablespoon salt
Soup Stock:
  5 cups water
  2 fish bouillon cubes
3 tablespoons salad oil
⅔ teaspoon salt
Dash of pepper
Some parmesan cheese and chopped parsley

1 Mince the onion and garlic.
2 Skin the sac part of the squid and cut into 1 cm/½ inch-wide rings. Place the littleneck clams in a bowl with salted water to remove sand. Rub the shells together in order to thoroughly clean the clams.
3 Place 5 cups of water and the bouillon cubes in a pot and heat.
4 In a separate pot, heat the salad oil. Sauté the minced onions and garlic until they began to release their aromas. Add the unwashed rice and continue to sauté. (Pictures 1–2)
5 Add the squid, littleneck clams, and soup stock, as prepared in Step 3. Bring to a boil. Turn down the heat to low and continue to cook for 15–18 minutes. Stir occasionally.
(Pictures 3–4)
6 Season with salt and pepper. Place on individual plates. If desired, sprinkle with parmesan cheese and chopped parsley to taste.

Tomato Risotto

A refreshing Italian dish with tomatoes and a pleasant herbal aroma.

Makes 4 servings

250 g/8⅓ oz rice
¼ onion (40 g/1⅓ oz)
½ clove garlic
20 g/⅔ oz celery
10 g/⅓ oz large green onion or *poireau*
20 g/⅔ oz thinly sliced bacon
25 g/⅔ oz carrot
1 whole tomato
Soup Stock:
   5 cups water
   2 bouillon cubes
2 tablespoons butter
1 bay leaf
Dash of thyme
Dash of basil
200 g/7 oz canned tomatoes, cooked in water
1 teaspoon salt
Dash of pepper

1 Mince the onion and garlic. Thinly slice the celery and carrot into 1 cm/½ inch-square pieces. Cut the piece of large green onion into 1 cm/½ inch-wide pieces.

2 Chop the bacon into 8 mm/3 inch squares and quickly boil. Peel the tomato and remove and discard the seeds. Chop the tomato into 8 mm/3 inch cubes.

3 Mix Soup Stock in a pot and heat to thoroughly dissolve the bouillon cubes.

4 Melt the butter in a separate pot. Sauté the minced onions, garlic and chopped celery. Add the chopped bacon, carrots and tomato, and continue to sauté for a short time longer.

5 Add the unwashed rice and sauté. Add the bay leaf, thyme, basil and hot soup stock. Continue to cook for another 15 minutes while stirring occasionally. Add the canned tomatoes to the mixture, crushing them as you go. Continue to cook for 5 minutes over medium heat. Sprinkle with salt and pepper.

Mushroom Risotto

The combination of mushrooms and milk brings out the subtle flavors of this dish.

Makes 4 servings
250 g/8½ oz rice
⅓ onion (50–60 g/2 oz.)
80 g/2⅔ oz brown mushrooms
6 fresh *shiitake* mushrooms
2 packs *shimeji* mushrooms (200 g/7 oz)
Soup Stock:
   5 cups water
   2 bouillon cubes
3 tablespoons butter
½ cup white wine
⅔ teaspoon salt
Dash of pepper
1 cup fresh cream
Some parmesan cheese

1 Mince the onion.
2 Remove and discard the stems of the brown mushrooms and *shiitake* mushrooms, and cut into 2–3 mm/⅛ inch-wide slices. Remove and discard the bottom of the stems of the *shimeji* mushrooms and break apart each bunch into 2–3 smaller bunches.
3 Mix the water and bouillon cubes in a pot and heat to thoroughly dissolve the bouillon cubes.
4 In a separate pot, melt the butter and sauté the minced onions until they become translucent. Add the mushrooms prepared in Step 2 and continue to sauté while stirring occasionally.
5 Add the rice and continue to sauté until it becomes translucent. Add the white wine and cook until all of the wine has been absorbed by the rice. Add the hot soup stock and continue to cook for an additional 15 minutes, while stirring occasionally.
6 Season with salt and pepper. Mix in fresh cream and cook for short time. Place on individual plates and sprinkle with parmesan cheese to taste.

Sunomono/Vinegared Dishes

Sunomono is a type of vinegared dish which is essential to Japanese cooking. Pickled turnips with lemon and *kohaku-namasu*, sweet pickled carrots and *daikon*, are commonly served at the time of the New Year.

Pickled Turnips Flavored with Lemon
(*Kabu no remon zuke*)

Makes 4–6 servings
5 small turnips, peeled and cut into round slices; ½ tbsp salt; 5 lemon slices, peeled; 1 piece ginger, cut into julienne; Seasoning: 3 tbsp vinegar, 1⅓ tbsp sugar, ¼ tsp salt, ½ tsp sesame oil

1 Sprinkle the turnips with salt and let stand until they become limp. Quickly rinse and squeeze to remove excess water.
2 Mix Seasoning in a bowl. Add the turnips, ginger, lemon and stir well to allow the flavors to mingle.

Sweet Pickled Cabbage and Cucumber
(*Kyabetsu to kyuri no amazu zuke*)

Makes 4 servings
200 g/7 oz of cabbage, 2 slender cucumbers, 5 cm/2 inch-long piece carrot, 1½ tsp salt, 1 red hot pepper, 2 tbsp salad oil, 5 tbsp sugar, 4 tbsp vinegar

1 Cut cabbage into 5 cm/⅕ inch squares. Cut cucumber into 5 cm/⅕ inch-long sections, and then slice lengthwise into thin pieces.
2 Cut carrot into 1 cm/½ inch-wide strips. Place in boiling water for 2–3 seconds. Remove and allow to cool.
3 Place cabbage, cucumbers and carrot in a large bowl. Sprinkle with salt and mix. Place a weight, such as a plate, over the bowl and let stand for 15–20 minutes. When the vegetables become limp, squeeze to remove the excess liquid.
4 Cut pepper in half diagonally and remove the seeds. Quickly fry in salad oil. Then add sugar and vinegar and bring to a boil. Pour this vinegar mixture over the vegetables prepared in step 3. Let stand to allow the flavors to mingle.

Daikon Radish and Carrot Pickles
Daikon to ninjin no namasu)

Makes 4-6 servings
400 g/1 lb *daikon* radish, peeled and julienned; 50 g/2 oz carrot, peeled and julienned; ⅔ tbsp salt; Vinegar Dressing: 3 tbsp sugar, 3 tbsp vinegar, ⅗ tsp salt

1 Place the *daikon* and carrot in a bowl and sprinkle with salt. Let stand for 15 minutes. Squeeze out excess liquid.
2 Mix together Vinegar Dressing. Add the vegetables prepared in Step 1 and mix together well. Let stand to allow the flavors to mingle.

Cucumber and Seaweed Vinegared Salad
(*Kyuri to wakame no sunomono*)

Makes 2 servings
2 cucumbers, dash of salt, 30 g/1 oz *wakame* seaweed soaked in water; Vinegar Dressing: 4 tbsp vinegar, 1 tbsp sugar, 2 tsp soy sauce, ¼ tsp salt

1 Cut cucumbers crosswise into thin slices. In a bowl, rub cucumber with salt until limp. Squeeze out excess liquid. Squeeze out excess water and cut *wakame* into 2 cm/⅔ inch wide strips.
2 Combine Dressing and cucumber and seaweed. Pour ⅓ of the Dressing over the vegetables and squeeze to remove excess liquid. Before serving, dress the vegetables with the remaining Dressing.

Japanese-Style Radish Pickles
(*Radisshu no wafu pikurusu*)

Makes 4 servings
20 radishes, 1 tsp salt, Vinegar Dressing: 4 tbsp vinegar, 3 tbsp *mirin*, ¼ tsp salt

1 Remove and discard the roots and leaves from radishes. Quickly rinse and pat dry. Sprinkle salt over the radishes and mix well. Let stand for 30–40 minutes.
2 In a bowl, mix together Vinegar Dressing. Place the radishes in the bowl. Let stand for 20–30 minutes to allow the flavors to mingle.

Japanese Omelet (*Tamago yaki*)

Makes 4 servings
4 eggs
3 tablespoons *dashi* stock
1½ tablespoons sugar
½ teaspoon soy sauce
Dash of salt
1½ tablespoons salad oil

1 In a bowl, beat the eggs together with the *dashi*, sugar, soy sauce and salt.
2 Heat a rectangular omelet pan. Add oil and thoroughly coat the pan. With a small ball of paper towels, wipe away the excess oil. Set aside the paper towel ball. Pour ⅓ of the beaten egg mixture into the pan. As the egg mixture begins to set, gently stir the uncooked parts with chopsticks. When the egg is half cooked, roll it up and place it at one side of the pan.
3 Using the paper towel ball, coat the cooking surface with oil. Pour half of the remaining egg mixture into the pan. When the egg is half cooked, roll it up, with the first omelet as the center. Prepare the remaining egg mixture in the same way. Use a bamboo rolling mat to shape the omelet nicely and then cut it into 1.5 cm/½ inch wide pieces.

Hamburger Patties

Makes 4 servings
50 g/2 oz ground beef
150 g/5 oz ground pork
  ½ large onion, minced
  ½ tablespoon salad oil
  ⅔ cup bread crumbs
  3 tablespoons milk
  1 scant teaspoon salt
  Dash of pepper
  ½ tablespoon soy sause
2 tablespoons butter, softened
1 egg
2 tablespoons salad oil

1 To make the hamburger patties: sauté the minced onion in ½ tablespoon of salad oil until brown. Let cool. Mix the bread crumbs with milk to moisten.
2 Mix the beef and pork together with the onion and bread crumbs and season with salt, pepper and soy sauce. Add the butter and egg and mix together with your hands. Divide into four patties.
3 Heat a frying pan and add 2 tablespoons of salad oil. Place the patties into the pan, making a slight indentation in the middle of each patty. Cook over high heat for 30 seconds. Lower the heat and continue cooking for 3–4 minutes. Turn the patties over and cook over high heat for 30 seconds. Add saké and lower the heat. Cook for an additional 3–4 minutes.

Glossary

Aburage, see Tofu, page 131

Ama-ebi (*botan-ebi* or *taraba-ebi*)
Sweet-tasting small shrimp.

Bouquet Garni
Savory herbs such as celery leaves, the stems of parsley, bay leaves, and thyme bundled together and tied with string. Bouquet garni are often used in French soups and stews.

Bracken(*zenmai*)
Zenmai is a savory herb, which can be used fresh, but dried *zenmai* yields better flavors when cooked. To reconstitute dried *zenmai*, soak in warm water overnight. Cook slowly over medium heat, then reduce the heat to low. Cook until soft and then set aside to cool.

Cha-shu
This is pork which has been grilled directly over a flame. It is used in Chinese cooking.

Ching-gêng-cai
A Chinese vegetable, the stems and leaves of which can be used in a variety of different dishes.

Chrysanthemum
Chrysanthemums are edible flowers. Rip the petals off, quickly boil in water with a dash of salt, then squeeze dry. Mix in with vinegared dishes or *aemono* dishes. Yellow chrysanthemums, called *kakinegiku*, are cultivated for eating. There are also processed chrysanthemums, called *kiku-nori*, which are steamed chrysanthemums formed into thin sheets then dried.

Cod Roe/*Tarako*
Cod roe is sold fresh, either salted or flavored with red chilli peppers.

Coriander, fresh
In Portuguese, coriander is called cilantro. Like celery and parsley, coriander is an annual lily. This savory herb is used often in China and India. In China, people call it *shang-cai*.

Daikon **Radish**
The root vegetable *daikon* is a member of the Cruciferae family and has been grown in Japan for centuries. The fresh radish can be grated, cooked, pickled or prepared as a salad. Dried radish can be reconstituted and used for vinegar pickles and in stir-fries.

Daikon **Sprouts/***Kaiwarena*
Kaiwarena are the sprouts of *daikon* and have the savory bitter taste of grated *daikon*. Used in salads and as garnishes.

Dashi **stock**
To make *dashi*, wipe a 10 cm/4 inch square piece of *konbu* with a towel and place it in a pot. Cover with 5 cups of water. Let stand for 10 minutes. Cook over medium heat and bring to a boil. Remove the *konbu*. Add 30 g/1 oz bonito flakes at once, when it comes to a boil again, take the pot from the heat. Strain. A good, prepared *dashi* on the market is Ajinomoto's Hon Dashi. Hon Dashi comes in a bottle and can be used whenever *dashi* stock is called for.

Dried Mushrooms, see *Hoshi-jiitake*, page 130

Dou-pan-jiang/**Chinese Brown Bean Paste**
A type of *miso* made from broad beans that contains hot chilli peppers. It has an exciting spiciness and is essential for Szechuan-style Chinese cooking.

Dried shrimp
Dried shrimp are used to add flavor in Chinese cooking. Before using, soak in plenty of warm water for half a day. Reconstituted shrimp can be frozen for instant use later.

Enoki **Mushrooms**
*Enok*i is a type of *nameko* mushroom which commonly grows on nettle trees and Japanese beech trees. *Enoki* mushrooms once grew only in the northeast part of the main island of Honshu, but today they are cultivated throughout Japan in bottles.

Flounder/*Hirame*

Flounder is a salt water fish which belongs to the Bothidae family. It looks similar to halibut and can reach lengths of up to 80 cm/32 inches.

Garam masala

Unique to Indian cooking, garam masala is a blend of the following spices: red pepper, black pepper, cloves, ginger, cardamon and cinnamon. One tablespoon of garam masala will add wonderful spiciness to any curry dish.

Gari/Sweet Pickled Ginger

Gari is ginger pickled in vinegar which is commonly served with sushi. To prepare *gari*, thinly slice ginger, quickly boil and let cool in water. Drain to remove the excess liquid and place in vinegar to pickle.

Gobo/Burdock root

Burdock root is a biennial compositae. It can grow as large as 7–8 cm/2–3 inches in diameter and 50–60 cm/20–24 inches in length. It is often included in *nimono* dishes for its wonderful crunchiness.

Green onion/*Negi*

Negi refers to the group of thick green onions in which only the white part is used, while *hanegi* refers to the type in which only the green part is used. There are other types of green onions including *asatsuki* (chives), which have long slender hollow stalks, and *wakegi* (tufted stone leeks), the bulbs of which separate from the base of the root, as well as Western varieties such as *poireau* and *echalote*.

Hanpen

Hanpen is made of ground white fish mixed with a sticky mountain potato called *yamaimo*. The mixture is placed in a shallow mold and boiled.

Hijiki

Hijiki belongs to the family of brown algae. Before cooking, dried *hijiki* must be reconstituted in water until soft.

Kabocha/Japanese pumpkin/Butternut squash

A small, round pumpkin-like squash with a dark green or black skin, the *kabocha* is full of vitamin A. It is used in *nimono*, *agemono*, and *mushimono* dishes.

Kamaboko/Fish Cakes

Kamaboko fish cakes are made from a mixture of ground fish and seasonings which is steamed or grilled. In the 14th and 15th centuries, these fish cakes were used in religious rituals.

Kampyo/Gourd Strips

Kampyo are long thin strips of dried gourd. To prepare *kampyo*, first rinse dried gourd strips and then sprinkle with a generous pinch of salt. Rub the strips together with your hands and rinse again. Place *kampyo* in boiling water and return to a boil. Quickly turn off the heat and drain in a colander.

Katakuriko/Rice Flour

Katakuriko is a silky starch which is refined from the bulb of the Adder's Tongue, a variety of lily. It is used to thicken and produce a very smooth sauce. Be sure to thoroughly dissolve *katakuriko* in two times the amount of water before adding to boiling liquid. Stir quickly.

Kimchee

Kimchee is a type of spicy Korean pickle made from cabbage, prepared salty vegetables such as *daikon* radish, cucumbers, onions, leeks, scallions and seafoods including fish and oysters.

Kinome

Kinome are the young leaves of the *sansho*, or Japanese pepper tree. They are used to garnish soups, as well as *nimono* and *yakimono* dishes. For *aemono* dishes, the leaves are ground.

Kobu Dashi Stock

To make *kobu dashi* stock, wipe a 10 x 15 cm/ 4 x 6 inch square of *konbu* clean with a towel. Soak it in 5 cups of water for 1–2 hours. Cook over medium heat, when bubbles start to come up, remove the *konbu*.

Kochujang

Kochujang, used in Korean cooking, is a type of *miso* which contains hot chilli pepper. It is made of *koji* and glutinous rice. It has a spicy but mild flavor with less saltiness than other types of *miso*.

Komatsuna

Komatsuna is a green-yellow vegetable grown in winter. It contains plenty of vitamin A, calcium and iron.

Konbu or *Kobu*

Sea kelp for making Japanese soup stock (*dashi*), or *nimono* dishes. Strips or rectangular sheets of cut *kobu*, *kiri-kobu*, are also available as well as *tororokobu*, a processed *konbu* in which many layers of *konbu* are compressed and then finely shaved.

Konnyaku

Konnyaku is a perennial belonging to the taro family. It is made from the bulb of the *konnyaku-imo*, or devil's tongue root.

Koya-dofu, see Tofu

Lotus root

Lotus root is a root vegetable which belongs to the water lily family.

Me-negi

Me-negi is a very thin young green onion.

Mirin/Sweet Rice Wine

Mirin is a sweet, thick cooking wine that is used in Japanese cooking to sweeten dishes.

Miso/Soybean Paste

Miso is made from steamed soybeans which are mixed with *koji* (a yeast-like mold made from rice and barley) and fermented. Various types of *miso* are available. They are classified according to color, the type of *koji* used, and their saltiness.

Mitsuba/Trefoil

The perennial *mitsuba*, in the family of Japanese parsley, is a savory herb prized for its aroma and vibrant green color.

Mochi-gome

This is a type of glutinous rice.

Murame

Murame is the bud of the red *shiso* plant (*aka-jiso*). *Murame* is used as a garnish for *sashimi* and in clear soups.

Namplaa Fish Sauce

This fish sauce, an essential ingredient in Southeast Asian cooking, is made by fermenting fish in salty water and then skimming off the liquid. *Namplaa* is the name given to the sauce in Thailand. In Vietnamese, it is referred to as *Nuoc Nam*. If unavailable, light soy sauce (*usukuchi shoyu*) may be substituted.

Nori

Red algae is strained and dried to form very thin rectangular sheets, called *nori*. Dried *nori* contains high quality protein, minerals and vitamins A and B_1. People enjoy both the aroma and flavor of *nori*.

Quail eggs

Quail eggs contain more vitamin B_2 and iron than chicken eggs.

Rice Vinegar

Vinegars can be made from a variety of ingredients, such as rice and other grains, or fruits such as apples and grapes. Vinegar is usually made naturally, but sometimes chemicals are used in the process and this vinegar is then called *goseisu*. The rice vinegar which is generally used in Japanese cooking is mild due to the natural method used to make it. The flavor of vinegar changes with the addition of salt and sugar; this combination is used to dress *aemono* dishes.

Saké

Japanese wine made from rice is commonly referred to as saké. Saké which is brewed purely from rice is classified as *seishu*, meaning pure liquor. Saké which is brewed using chemicals is called *goseishu*, meaning compound liquor. *Seishu* is the type of saké commonly used in cooking.

Salmon Roe/*Ikura or ikra*
Salmon roe or sea bass roe preserved in salt.

Scallions
A type of onion belonging to the Ascalon family. Scallions, with their strong and unique aroma, are often used in Chinese cooking.

Sea bream/*Tai*
Sea bream is a salt water fish which belongs to the Sparidae family. The best sea bream are said to be those that weigh about 2 kg/4 lbs and which are as long as 30 cm/12 inches.

Sesame oil
Sesame oil contains 40% linolic acid and oilen acid, thus protecting it from oxidation and loss of flavor. A dash of sesame oil added to regular cooking oil adds richness. It is excellent to use for making fried rice and pickles.

Sesame Salt/*Goma-shio*
To prepare sesame salt, roast ½ cup of sesame seeds and ⅔ cup of salt together in a heavy bottomed frying pan. Be careful not to burn the mixture. Sesame salt is readily available in supermarkets and is sold in jars. Keep it free from moisture.

Seven-Spice Pepper
Seven-spice pepper is made from equal portions of the following seven ingredients: hot red pepper, *sansho* pepper, ground orange peel, sesame seeds, hemp seeds, poppy seeds and rapeseed.

Shiitake Mushrooms
Nama-jiitake: Fresh *shiitake*
Fresh *shiitake* mushrooms are used for *nimono* dishes in which ingredients are simmered together in a pot for long time; *nabemono*, a style of cooking in which ingredients are usually cooked in a ceramic pot; tempura; and *shirumono*, or soup dishes. To keep the mushrooms fresh, wrap them in a wet paper towel, put in a plastic bag and store in the refrigerator.

Hoshi-jiitake: Dried *shiitake*
Dried *shiitake* mushrooms must be reconstituted before they can be used. Soak them in cold or warm water for about 30 minutes. The soaking liquid may be reserved and used for *dashi*, or Japanese soup stock.

Shimeji Mushrooms
Shimeji mushrooms grow in bunches in wet thickets. The mushrooms are small and have thin stems. They are used in soups, *nimono* dishes and *nabemono* dishes.

Shishito Pepper or *Shishi Togarashi*
A type of small-sized, mild Japanese green pepper.

Shirasuboshi
Shirasuboshi are young anchovies which have been boiled in salty water and then dried.

Shirataki
These fine noodles are formed from *konnyaku*.

Shiso
The *shiso*, or beefsteak plant, is an annual. There are red *shiso* plants (*aka-jiso*) and green *shiso* plants (*ao-jiso*). The *shiso* plant, which contains many vitamins, is a commonly used ingredient and adds a refreshing aroma and color to a dish. Perialdehyde is the component of the aroma. Various parts of the *shiso* plant are used: the buds or *me-jiso* (referred to as *murame* for red *shiso* plant buds, and *aome* for green *shiso* plant buds), the flowers (*hana-jiso*), the spikes (*ho-jiso*) and the seeds (*mi-jiso*).

Snow peas
Snow peas are a type of annual legume. Select young soft pods for cooking.

Soy Sauce/*Shoyu*
This common ingredient is made from soybean and flour (*koji*) which is then mixed with salted

water, fermented and filtered. Dark soy sauce (*koikuchi*) is commonly used in everyday cooking. Light soy sauce (*usukuchi*) brings out the flavor of vegetables without turning them too dark a color.

Suan-Tai: Garlic sprouts

Tofu
There are two types of tofu. One is *kinugoshi*, the other is called *momengoshi*. *Momen dofu* is made by first grinding up soy beans and cooking them. Then they are filtered through a cloth to separate the soy milk from the *okara*, or soybean husks. A coagulant is then added to the soy bean milk. As the tofu becomes solid, it is transferred to a box lined with cotton cloth and a weight is placed on top. *Kinugoshi dofu* is made with a thicker soy bean milk which is then solidified, without using weight.

Tofu, Deep-fried/Tofu Puff/*Aburage*
Aburage is deep-fried tofu. Tofu is cut into thin slices or bars, and then deep-fried in cooking oil. Store *aburage* in a plastic bag in the refrigerator.

Tofu, Dried/*Koya-dofu*
Koya-dofu is freeze-dried tofu. It originated with the Buddhist monks of Mt. Koya, who discovered this technique when they dried frozen tofu which had accidentally been left outside in the cold.

Tororokobu
A processed *konbu* product. See *konbu*, page 129.

Wakame Seaweed
Wakame belongs to the family of brown algae. To bring out the vibrant green of dried *wakame*, quickly soak in hot water after reconstituting. *Wakame* is used in *miso* soup and *aemono*, or salad dishes.

Wasabi horseradish
Yama-wasabi, mountain horseradish, and *mizu-wasabi*, water horseradish, are grown in cool areas with clean water. Horseradish which is grown in a field is called *hata* (field) *wasabi* or *riku* (land) *wasabi*. *Wasabi* is usually grated or chopped into thread-like slivers. Powdered *wasabi* is also available and is prepared by mixing with a small amount of water. People enjoy its distinctive spiciness and aroma. For fresh *wasabi*, cut off the stem and peel only the part you are planning to grate at that time. To keep the remaining *wasabi* fresh, wrap in a wet paper towel, place in a plastic bag and store in the refrigerator.

Yaki nori/Toasted Seaweed
Yaki nori goes very well with Japanese rice dishes such as *donburi* and sushi. When *yaki nori* is used as the final touch to a dish, it is torn into small pieces or cut into thin strips with scissors to bring out its aroma.

Yukari
Finely chopped, salt-pickled red *shiso* leaves. Sundry then rub to release flavor.

Index for Recipes